Active Career Management

A Practical Guide to a Fast-Track Career Path for Business Professionals

By
Robert Wilson

Cover design by Kit Foster.

Edited by Madalyn Stone.

Table of Contents

Section 1

Building the Foundation while in School

Chapter 1: Maximizing Your Education

Being selective about where you focus your study time—in terms of what you study and how you study—is critical to getting the most benefit following graduation. This chapter discusses techniques to use your school work to your advantage in interviews and on the job.

Chapter 2: Goal Setting and Management

Use this step-by-step process to help you clearly define your ultimate career goals and build a "career map" (starting with your final goal in mind). This process will help you set appropriate milestones (based on your goals), assess your performance and adjust your plans as necessary to keep on pace with your overall career objective.

Chapter 3: Building a Network

Discover the importance of a strong professional network, as well as whom to target for your network, how to gain supporters, and how to best maintain your network as your career evolves.

Chapter 4: Internships

Gaining a strong internship opportunity prior to graduation is very important. This chapter provides advice on how to obtain one and how to approach internships to derive maximum benefit.

Chapter 5: Selecting a Company

It is important to balance company recognition and the long-term, career flexibility that this might provide—particularly in a first job—against specific learning, development, and on-the-job experiences within a particular company. A practical approach is shared here.

Chapter 6: Getting an Interview (Developing and Distributing Your Resume)

There are several critical elements to effectively developing a compelling resume, as well as different methods for putting your resume in the hands of employers. Whether you are in school or have already started your career, this chapter provides a practical approach to getting an interview.

Chapter 7: Interviewing

Preparing for any interview should involve researching prospective employers, developing expected interview questions and responses, as well as utilizing techniques for compelling communication that will help you stand out from other candidates. This chapter provides a step-by-step approach to help you prepare for each of these areas.

Chapter 8: Selecting a Job

Four major factors are shared that should be considered when selecting a job. They will help you systematically assess a new opportunity and its benefits against your long-term career goals, ensuring that a given career opportunity provides appropriate flexibility, compensation, and responsibilities.

Section 2

Early to Midcareer Management

Chapter 9: How and Why to Impress Customers Early

This chapter highlights the importance of impressing customers early from a career development and advancement standpoint and provides practical methods to increase your likelihood of success.

Chapter 10: Building and Exploiting Exposure to Gain Sponsorship

A step-by-step approach is provided to help identify ideal as well as realistic sponsor targets. Further, a strategy for taking advantage of exposure opportunities and also proactively "creating" exposure opportunities is shared.

Chapter 11: Managing Perceptions

Understanding how you are perceived and building a process for continuously monitoring and ensuring that you thoughtfully manage your approach, behaviors, and actions to ensure you and your work are positively and credibly received is very important. This chapter provides a framework to help.

Chapter 12: Building Your Resume While at Work

Building a resume is often the outcome of an individual's work. However, a different approach is discussed here—starting with the end objective and working back to ensure that you select the optimal roles and work to help you create an "ideal" resume.

Chapter 13: Core Competencies and Competitive Advantages

A method for determining your core competencies and competitive advantages is provided along with advice on how to best use this knowledge to advance your career.

Chapter 14: When to Consider an MBA

A step-by-step approach for evaluating the value of an MBA and comparing this against other career alternatives is provided in this chapter.

Chapter 15: Why and When to Change Jobs

Knowing whether and ultimately when to consider changing employers can be a very difficult decision. A logical process is presented to help you thoughtfully evaluate career progression prospects at your current company versus other prospective employers, as well as thinking about when a change might be most advantageous.

Chapter 16: Continuous Performance Assessment and Management

To ensure that you are making desired progress toward your career objectives, it is helpful to have a process for tracking, evaluating, and modifying your performance. This chapter provides a simple framework for checking and adjusting your current-year performance, while considering implications for longer-term career management.

Chapter 17: Some Final Thoughts

This short, final chapter provides some brief, concluding advice, as well as useful resources that might be helpful in your active career management process.

Preface

Why I Wrote this Book and How It Can Help You

I started out my working career more than a decade ago, no different from a lot of my peers coming out of school in the late 90s. I graduated from a respectable university with a bachelor's degree and a reasonable grade point average. The job market was fairly strong, with many companies investing heavily to minimize Y2K issues, followed by a tech boom that was fueled largely by the expansion of the Internet and the dot.com phenomenon. I received several offers for employment and ultimately went to work for a major consumer products company as a cost analyst in the division where I had completed a summer internship the prior year. From there, I went on to join a financial software start-up company during the technology boom, which soared then fell like so many others during that era. Desiring greater stability, I took a job as a senior cost analyst at another large consumer products company in one of their manufacturing plants.

Building on the experiences from the early part of my career at my first employer and the software start-up, I navigated quickly through several roles in different parts of this new company, gaining exposure and sponsorship that ultimately led to my becoming one of the youngest executives at the company. Throughout this journey, I effectively surpassed all of my peers, friends, and graduating class in terms of responsibilities, title, and compensation. Many of these individuals clearly had stronger educational backgrounds, greater work experiences, broader networks, rich family histories of business successes, and equally ambitious career objectives.

Reflecting on why my career moved at a faster pace than that of my peers—despite being "disadvantaged" on the surface by traditional predictors (such as education, networks, standardized test scores, etc.)—there are a combination of factors that I believe ultimately led to my successes. Over the past few years, I began to organize my thoughts around what has worked for me and why—as well as how the same techniques could work effectively for many others. My conclusion is that there is really nothing innately unique about my skills or particular situation. However, the methods that I used and the sequence in which I employed them, from my time in college through my most recent role as a Division CFO for a multibillion dollar global business unit, are unique.

As my career trajectory began to accelerate, many of my colleagues and peers began to come to me for career advice. Like me, most of these individuals had received plenty of prior advice on what they should do to accelerate their careers. However, similar to the advice I had received throughout my academic and working career, most of these individuals indicated that the perspectives they had been provided were fairly one-dimensional and tainted by others' *perceptions of success* based on their own careers.

Interestingly, what I found was that there really was no single comprehensive resource to provide highly motivated individuals with practical guidance on how to effectively manage a career. Whereas most educational programs focus on technical and occasionally leadership skills—and there are a multitude of books about organizational management and leadership—there is surprisingly little guidance available regarding career management and navigation.

Though not an exhaustive resource, this book will provide readers with a systematic guide with specific and actionable techniques and approaches that worked very effectively for me and others I have coached over several years in a number of different organizations. If applied consistently and with an open mind, the tools in this book should help you actively manage your career and achieve your professional goals, starting with activities and areas to focus on while you are still in school, and continuing through the early years of your career.

Is this Book for You?

I would like to begin by clearly stating that this book is *not* for everyone. While I am very confident that the approaches and techniques outlined here can be implemented effectively and to varying degrees by a relatively wide audience, the extent of success will require a strong work ethic and a consistent and active employment of the recommended approaches not just when convenient, but as something you incorporate into your ongoing, daily work plan. Some of the changes required in order to move your career onto the fast-track may be as subtle as ensuring you gain increased exposure to key customers. However, many of the changes will require greater sacrifice and a commitment to focusing and allocating your available time to those areas (as outlined in this book) that will get you recognized for the right things by the right people and at the optimal time in your career.

As you become comfortable using the techniques in this book, you will need to also get more comfortable with increasingly faster promotions, additional career opportunities, and greater compensation!

Active versus Passive Career Management: Why Some Careers Soar and Others Stall

Quite early in my career, I became interested in watching and understanding the relative speed of career progression for individuals with seemingly consistent skills, tenure, and performance. I was curious about what it was that appeared to make some employees rise to the top of an organization, whereas others with skills apparently quite comparable were on very different trajectories, despite similar desires for advancement.

Clearly, there is a certain fundamental level of technical competence, leadership capability, and work ethic that is required to advance within an organization. However, these "traditional" factors on their own cannot be consistently relied upon to advance one's career at an accelerated rate. In discussing this phenomenon with peers and other experienced employees, it was common for intelligence, connections, or corporate political awareness to be cited as the key to accelerated career progression. However, upon closer assessment, it became apparent to me that these were *not* the major drivers in most situations.

In reality, what I found was a theme that was much simpler and honestly quite logical, but not often cited or understood. The concept is something that I refer to as "active" versus "passive" career management and involves two very different approaches. To use an automotive analogy, "active" career managers could be described as the drivers of a car with a map and a clear sense for where they want to be and by what time. By contrast, "passive" career managers could be thought of as passengers in a vehicle that is headed in the same direction, but without clarity as to where or when the car will be stopping, and without knowing the exact final destination. This example may seem a bit extreme, but it highlights the very different attitudes and approaches taken by individuals as it relates to their careers. Which person do you think is more likely to achieve rapid career advancement—the "active" or "passive" individual? As simple as this might seem, I have consistently seen very talented individuals lose out on promotions and great career opportunities simply because they did not think to manage their careers in the same fashion that they managed the projects or businesses that they supported.

To illustrate this concept further, let's look at two individuals, Joe and Ann, whose names are fictitious but whose stories are not. Both Joe and Ann attended similar schools, started their careers at approximately the same time, and had progressed into their early careers at equivalent rates, largely as a result of strong technical skills, coupled with good leadership abilities. However, after a couple of years on comparable career progressions, Ann began to receive numerous promotional opportunities, whereas Joe was offered more lateral transfers than promotional assignments.

So, what drove the stagnation of Joe's career and the acceleration of Ann's? On the surface, the answer was not clear. Joe had moved several times with the company and had taken on new opportunities whenever they were offered to him—regardless of what the job entailed. Furthermore, each of his supervisors had positive things to say about Joe's work. In fact, he had a reputation for being the "go to" resource that could solve almost any issue, regardless of complexity or other work demands. Ann had similarly favorable feedback, but hadn't moved as many times and was a bit more selective about the roles that she had taken on—even though she had been advised by some of her managers that many of the roles she ultimately turned down would provide "good experiences" that she really should consider. Even so, just four years into her career, Ann was considerably ahead of Joe.

Upon closer inspection of each of their most recent career moves, the progression of Ann versus Joe became much more obvious—and clearly resulted from Joe's "passive" approach to managing his career, compared to Ann's very "active" methods. While I don't believe that either Joe or Ann recognized that they were taking "active" or "passive" approaches to their careers, their actions clearly could be categorized into these very different classifications. While Joe was willing to take on any activity that his manager and other customers requested and did it with excellence, Ann was much more selective. Before starting any new project, Ann first tried to assess what was going to be valued most by the new division manager Mike, who was not her immediate supervisor, but who was an indirect customer of much of the work that she did. Mike had a reputation for developing and recognizing "up-and-coming" talent, and he prided himself on identifying future leaders and sharing his findings with other senior leaders. While Ann attended to each of the requests from her supervisor, she allocated a disproportionate amount of time to the requests that she believed would end up having exposure to Mike.

6

Further, she was careful to assemble the information in a way that was very clear and concise—essentially, "executive friendly"—while still having the necessary supporting details to satisfy her direct manager's objectives. This extra time investment resulted in Ann getting the opportunity to present some of her findings and recommendations directly to Mike, who was very impressed and shared his favorable interactions with other senior leaders.

By contrast, Joe appeared to be prioritizing his work almost entirely on the level of importance dictated by his direct manager. Joe made the fairly typical assumption that if his manager was satisfied with his work, then new opportunities and advancement would happen naturally. What Joe did not appreciate was that his current supervisor lacked credibility with senior leadership. On top of that, the information that Joe prepared for his supervisor (while in the format requested), lacked the organization to be readily shared with senior leaders. Learning this, it was not surprising to hear that Joe had not received much exposure to senior leadership in his four years with the company. Furthermore, given the importance of senior leadership sponsorship required for promotions, Joe's lack of recent advancement was almost to be expected.

While this example refers to "active" versus "passive" management of one's career once in a job, the illustration is equally—and potentially even more relevant—during school, before starting a professional role in an organization. The classes you select, the study habits you employ, the contacts that you make, the summer jobs or internships that you hold, and the process that you use for interviewing and in selecting a company, can all be contemplated in a similar manner. While the playing field

7

may not feel level (and, in fact, it probably is not), the approach you take to each of these areas can dramatically slant the odds of career success in your favor.

As you navigate through each of these stages of progression, beginning while in school and continuing through your early career, there are five elements to consistently keep in mind as an "active" manager of your career, as follows: 1) a clear awareness of the most critical opportunities and actions that will be valued most heavily by those individuals who will have the greatest impact on your career; 2) perspective on who those individuals are who are most likely to positively impact your career; 3) an understanding of how to best gain exposure to these individuals and showcase your work in an impactful way; 4) a consistent and focused allocation of time to exploit these opportunities; and 5) a carefully considered road map with milestones for where you want to be and by when that is documented and referenced periodically. (Each of these elements will be explored further throughout the book.)

In thinking through the example of Joe versus Ann, it is clear that Ann was following at least four of the five aforementioned elements—and the results showed. By contrast, Joe was not "actively" managing his career and was, at best, adhering to maybe one of these "active" career management elements.

To maximize the probability of your success, you will need to take ownership for each element of the process, systematically mapping out each future move, and actively steering toward specific and logical milestones in your career journey, keeping each of the five elements outlined above clearly in mind.

8

How to Use this Book

This book was designed to be a road map that can be used to navigate through the career maze more effectively, starting with college and continuing through the early stages of your career. However, I recognize that each reader is at a different point on his or her career path. To accommodate this, a brief description of each chapter has been included in the table of contents to help you decide where to start.

If you have gotten this far in the book, you should have an appreciation for the importance of taking an "active" approach to managing your career—which would ideally start early in your college years and continue throughout your working career.

If you are currently in school, I highly recommend reading all of the chapters in the book—each element will provide you with perspectives on what to expect once you begin your working career—some of which may influence your choices and decisions about classes, organizations, and even friends and colleagues. However, at a minimum, you should plan to complete the chapters on "Internships," "Selecting a Company," "Getting an Interview," "Interviewing," and "Selecting a Job"—all of which will be very important during your time in school and will have a direct bearing on where you begin your career.

For individuals who are just entering the workforce, or who have recently joined, you could skip directly to section 2: "Early to Midcareer Management". However, I would strongly advise reading the chapters on "Goal Setting and Management" and "Building a Network: Who to Know and Why" from Section 1, as the skills outlined in these chapters are as applicable to individuals already in the workforce as they are to those still in school. If you are at all contemplating a change in companies or going back to school at some point, I would highly recommend going through section 1: "Building the Foundation while in School," which will provide recommendations on where to focus your time and resources and provide valuable perspectives on how to considerably increase your probability of success with job prospecting and interviewing.

No matter where you are in your own personal career journey, I am confident that the concepts and recommendations outlined in this book will provide you with valuable perspectives and principles that will enable you to accelerate your pace of career growth.

Section 1: Building the Foundation while in School

College is clearly the place to start building the foundation for the career that you want—and to provide the launching pad for accelerated success. This section of the book is designed to provide advice and recommendations on how to most effectively approach your time in school—with some of the chapters also having clear applicability for individuals already in the workforce (particularly chapters 2 and 3; chapters 6, 7, and 8 will also have direct applicability if you are in the workforce and are contemplating a change in employers).

This section begins with guidance on where to best allocate your study time—how to study and then apply your studies in a manner that will yield the most benefit from a career standpoint. I provide guidance about how to set clear and measurable career goals (starting with the end in mind), along with developing specific milestones, tracking, and assessment. This discussion evolves into describing the importance of a professional network, how to cultivate key relationships, and how to maintain them as your career progresses. I then discuss the sometimes underestimated value of strong internships, and give advice on how to approach them to ensure you extract maximum value from this investment. I briefly explore selecting a prospective employer and the implications on long-term career flexibility. I talk about the development of an effective resume in detail, along with methods for getting your resume in the hands of employers. This is followed by a chapter on proven but infrequently used methods to prepare for and to "stand-out" from other candidates in any interview. Finally, a structured job selection process is shared to ensure that you carefully consider new opportunities with regard to long-term career goals, and that you appropriately evaluate job flexibility, compensation, and responsibilities.

Chapter 1
Maximizing Your Education

If you are currently in school or are thinking about going back to school, you are in a perfect position to build a rock-solid foundation for future career success. Aside from choosing a major that aligns with your particular career aspirations and focusing on achieving a reasonable grade point average, there are several other factors you should carefully consider. This includes *what to study, how to study*, and *how to use* what you study. You may believe that you already know how to study, how to get acceptable grades, and ultimately, how to apply your knowledge. However, the *approach* you take to each of these areas will have a profound effect on your lasting comprehension and ability to effectively apply the right knowledge while in the workforce versus just on an examination. It is likely that the approach I am recommending will require not only a reallocation of your time but also potentially more of it. With that said, this "investment" will help you enhance your critical thinking skills as they relate to problem solving and strategy development en route to a much stronger career foundation.

What to Study

In my working experience, I would argue that there were really only four or five classes that I took at the college

13

level that provided most of the critical skills required to be effective in my field of work. Perhaps more interesting and ultimately more compelling is that I had a pretty good sense of what those classes were while I was taking them.

Desiring a career in corporate finance, I majored in finance at the University of Wisconsin. For me, the key classes included basic algebra (learned this as a freshman in high school), introductory finance, financial markets, real estate, cost accounting, and basic statistics. Despite the focus on numbers within my job in finance, most of the math isn't overly complex—a strong understanding of algebraic equations (the ability to write and dissect them) is really all that is needed. The other coursework from this list really provided the foundation for a core understanding of financial markets and instruments, capital project analysis, cost accounting methods and techniques, and statistical analysis. Interestingly, I mentioned a real estate course as a key class for me, even though I do not work in this field. It turned out that the real estate curriculum at Wisconsin had a heavy emphasis on financial simulation and spreadsheet modeling, which provided an incredibly useful foundation for much of the work that has been critical to my development and professional advancement.

I should caveat this by mentioning that I definitely appreciate the benefits that I received from all of the other coursework that I completed, which no doubt have helped to make me a well-rounded individual and ultimately have contributed to my success. However, the point that I want to make is that while you are in school, it is really critical that you keep the end objective in mind. (Consider what area you ultimately want to work in, which courses will be most critical to your success in this field, and what you expect you will need and be able to apply

14

from each of them.) To the extent that you have the ability to select from different courses or instructors, you owe it to yourself to do the due diligence and research the content of different course syllabi and to gather feedback on approaches to content provided by different professors.

Similar to my taking real estate courses that I believed would help augment my finance education, do not simply limit yourself to coursework provided by your major if there are other classes that you believe will benefit you significantly after you graduate from school.

Whenever possible, gather feedback from other individuals who you respect that are already working in your field of study. (It is ideal if these individuals also happen to be at the level to which you aspire.) This can be useful to understand what skills are most critical to success and where they would recommend placing extra focus. This will also help you to determine whether you have any gaps in your studies that need to be filled prior to leaving school. (For those of you already working in your field or with relevant prior working experience, you may already know the answers to these questions.) For me, advanced spreadsheet modeling is one such example of a unique skill required to be successful in my field that was not heavily emphasized in college. I did have the basics from my real estate coursework and some computer classes, but the level of sophistication needed was a bit of a surprise to me. Recognizing this in advance of my graduation may have changed my focus to turn this into a strength sooner.

As you identify those "core" classes or skills that will be critical to your future success after graduation, I would highly recommend that you treat them differently from other coursework. This applies to how you study for

15

exams, as well as how thoughtful you are in considering the application of this knowledge to scenarios outside of school. In order to get the most out of your education and exploit this to its fullest in your career, you will need to retain as much of the critical knowledge as possible and understand it in a complete and holistic manner so that you will be able to properly apply it in your specific work environment.

How to Study

Admittedly, there are "core" courses that are truly of maximum value for career success outside of college, but *how* an individual studies for these courses can have a major impact on the value gained as a result of taking them. Too frequently, I have seen individuals assume that grades are the ultimate measure for understanding as it relates to specific coursework, school, and for some— intelligence in general. Grades are clearly important— they are one of the most objective measures employers have when evaluating potential employees, particularly for internships when there is little work experience to showcase. However, it is my experience that the level of understanding and the lasting comprehension of useful and actionable information outside of academia between two people with identical grades can differ dramatically. My belief is this has to do with the testing style and, more importantly, the studying method.

Although potentially effective for some test taking, I would generally discourage brute force memorization as a mechanism for learning, especially in "core" courses that contain critical material that you will need to know to be successful in your profession. A generally more effective and lasting method for long-term comprehension involves a more integrated, holistic approach that requires mapping out the key relationships between all of the variables (to be clear—this isn't just for math courses), understanding the key drivers of each variable in the equation, what the output means relative to the different inputs, and how to react to this in a real-world environment. A simple example of where a holistic comprehension is much more valuable (and generally longer lasting) than a memorization method would be the different use and interpretation of financial ratios in my field of study and work. One ratio that is commonly considered (and tested in finance and accounting courses) is "days of inventory outstanding" (or DIO for short).

In simple mathematical terms,

$$DIO = \text{average inventory \$ value / cost of sales per day}$$

This measure provides a simple indicator for the number of days of production currently sitting in inventory. Memorizing the above equation or the interpretation of DIO as "the number of days of production currently sitting in inventory" may be all that is needed for a typical college examination. However, to be useful and ensure proper interpretation when used in industry, it would be important to understand numerous other factors related to this metric. For example, DIO represents the number of "days" based on $s, which includes not just finished goods for sales but also ingredients, work-in-process inventory, and manufacturing spare parts. Therefore, it is likely that the "actual" days of completed inventory (or finished goods) for sale in the factory warehouse is significantly less than the traditional DIO metric would suggest.

Further, DIO metrics can be impacted by inventory revaluations, production mix, sales mix, cost of sales changes, and other factors.

This is just one example, but the point is that if you believe the course's content will be of significant value to you after your examinations are completed, I would strongly suggest you modify your approach to studying for the course to ensure holistic, longer-term retention. If you can rapidly recall and apply the critical knowledge from school in your job situation, this will ultimately increase your effectiveness at work and improve your likelihood of accelerated career progression.

How to *Use* What You Study

This is really an extension of the discussion around *how to study*—which addresses the need to consider more than just what will be on the test if you want to ensure long-term comprehension of course material. However, this section will likely involve taking your studying to completely new levels—not just the time invested, but rather the value that is created from the investment. I would challenge you to carefully consider how what you are studying could be used or applied to improve or ideally provide an "optimizing solution" at your current or a potential future employer. (By optimizing solution I mean one that is ideal. This will often require some thoughtful contemplation.) Project work often provides an avenue for pushing yourself to think about your studies in such a manner; that is, applying the theoretical concepts later in an actual job situation.

In my case, I was able to exploit knowledge from a statistics course project in this manner. Having worked in the School of Agriculture while attending the University of Wisconsin, I was aware of the significant data collected pertaining to crop yields, as well as numerous, additional factors impacting yields, such as temperature, rainfall, sunlight, and weed densities. Utilizing several historical databases from the School of Agriculture, I was able to develop a sizable, integrated database on what I believed would be the key predictors of crop yields. Leveraging the multiple regression concepts and software from a statistics class, I developed an algorithm that could predict crop yields based on key environmental factors. In addition to a very good grade on the project, the more critical result was an advanced—and more importantly—*applied understanding* of multiple regression and other related statistical modeling techniques. This project had the added benefit of generating interest in my work by faculty in the Horticulture Department, which resulted in an agricultural statistics internship the next summer.

For individuals enrolled in a college course while working at a company—whether you plan to continue at this employer or not—this may provide an excellent vehicle for applying an academic concept to a business problem. In some situations, you might even have the opportunity to reinforce your learning from a course by using it in project work or work you do while employed. My advice is to aggressively look for opportunities to take advantage of these types of situations while in school. The extra time investments will increase your comprehension and capabilities when you are in the workforce—and ultimately increase your chances for advancement and a bigger paycheck.

Chapter 2
Goal Setting and Management

Even before you start your full-time career, I recommend that you invest the time to clearly define your career goals. Start with the end in mind and work backward—this will ensure you are developing plans that align with your ultimate objectives. Initially, this may be a difficult task, since you will have many available and suitable opportunities to apply what you learned in school. However, by carefully breaking down your goals into manageable pieces, you can develop a logical plan and road map for success. This chapter outlines a practical six-step process to make goal setting and management more achievable.

Step 1: Understand and Clearly Define Your Long-Term Goals

Gaining an understanding of your *long-term* professional goals may be as simple as targeting the level in management that you ultimately want to achieve (e.g., vice president of sales at a Fortune 100 consumer products company, or partner at a boutique consulting firm, etc.). At this point in the process, you might want to target a few scenarios—part of the next step will be to flesh out the details of these long-term, strategic career targets to ensure they truly align with your expectations. Too often, I have seen individuals develop plans that are too short-term in nature. For example, while in school, your goals are often very focused on school. This is not surprising, since these goals are more tangible and reachable. However, the risk is that you are setting short-term goals that you ultimately achieve but do not lead to meeting your intended, long-term objectives. The key is to be willing to step back, be honest with yourself, and make sure that you are always keeping your long-term objectives in mind when developing more tactical goals and milestones.

Step 2: Refine and Build Out the Details of Your Long-Range Career Target

For each of the potential targeted career levels defined in step 1, you will want to next refine and build out the details of these targeted roles in terms of expected responsibilities, constructing something that may resemble a rough job description. Include compensation, travel, and working-hour expectations within the job description. (It is crucial that you are honest in your assessments of time requirements to achieve the roles and responsibilities to which you aspire in step 1, and carefully consider your desired level of commitment to work versus other personal objectives.) As you work through this summary, you should ask yourself whether this career target still aligns with your overall objectives. If it does not, you probably need to work back through step 1 and develop alternative job targets. If you are still aligned with your objective from step 1, the next step will involve validating your assumptions around your targeted career path.

Step 3: Validate Your Assumptions from Step 2

This important next step is to gain external validation of your assumptions about responsibilities, accountabilities, time investment and compensation for the role details you defined in step 2. The best method for validating your assumptions would be to speak directly with individuals currently employed in roles comparable to your targets. However, this scenario will not be realistic for many people. Therefore, annual reports and job boards should provide sufficient information to validate your assumptions. You may also find the career office in your school to be helpful in assembling this data.

If your targeted position is below that of a "C-level" executive (e.g., CEO, CFO, CIO, etc.), then I would recommend using the different Internet job boards available, such as Careerbuilder.com, Monster.com, 6figurejobs.com, theLadders.com, or others to search for titles similar to those you originally identified in step 1. Interestingly, LinkedIn.com may be another very useful resource for this, as it relates to gaining an appreciation for organizational structures and reporting relationships. Simplify search titles in order to maximize results (e.g., "vice president sales"). (However, recognize that titles are often not comparable between companies, particularly those with significant differences in organizational size, scope, and complexity. Keep this in mind when attempting to validate your assumptions.) After sorting through the relevant listings and associated job descriptions, you should have a better sense for whether your targeted job level and associated responsibilities, accountabilities, and compensation are aligned.

If your desired job level is that of a C-level executive, then you will not likely find as much success benchmarking by using Internet job sites, particularly if you are interested in a larger corporation. For these roles, I would recommend using company annual reports as a resource, although they will not provide you with the same detail as a specific job description. However, they should provide some perspective on likely responsibility levels in terms of scope, scale, and compensation. Start by identifying companies by size and in the industry where you are interested. Most publicly traded companies provide annual reports on their websites. Yahoo finance is also a good resource, where historical Securities and Exchange Commission filings are generally available, including summaries of key executives, their associated responsibilities, and compensation levels.

Step 4: Map Out a Targeted Career Path

After you have solidified your long-term job target, the next step is to map out a career path that gets you from the targeted long-term job objective back to your current position (this applies whether you are currently in the workforce or still in school). This task may seem tedious, but it is actually quite logical and will ensure you have specific short-, mid-, and long-term milestones that will allow you to check and adjust your plans in a timely manner to keep you on track to achieve your ultimate career goals.

Identifying the logical levels between a likely entry level position and your target job level may be a bit difficult, but it really doesn't need to be perfect. The key is to be able to give you a sense of what you will want to target in terms of career achievement milestones early in your career to ensure you are building the necessary foundation of experiences, capabilities, and leadership qualities to put yourself on the appropriate pace to attain your ultimate objective.

It may be helpful to again reference some of the different Internet job boards for different postings within a particular functional area to see if you can find any differences between your current role (if you are presently in the workforce) or likely starting role (upon graduation) and your targeted, long-range job role. (Be careful to select companies in the same industry and the same size for doing your benchmarks—size and industry will often dictate scale, complexity, and norms in terms of organizational design.) For career targets at the associate director, director, or vice president level, it is likely that you will have some success developing a reasonably accurate career map using job boards, LinkedIn.com profiles, and referencing others who you might know in the workforce. For C-level positions, the mapping may be a bit less transparent. However, many companies have executive profiles listed on their websites that include prior positions held by executives. This may be helpful to augment what you have already assembled from other sources. It is unlikely that you will be able to complete a perfect career map (as they are all a bit different). However, I would recommend that you make some educated assumptions where you are unclear. Generally, you might expect the following core levels at most medium- to large-sized corporations:

- *analyst or specialist*
- *senior analyst or senior specialist*
- *manager*

- *associate director*
- *director*
- *senior director*
- *vice president*
- *executive vice president*

Titles will clearly differ among organizations and functions. Further, some corporations will have greater or fewer levels just based on the organizational model they have chosen to follow. You will be able to refine these maps much more clearly after you start your career with a specific company. However, at this point, it is simply good to have some general perspective on the relative difficulty and key milestones required to attain your objective.

Step 5: Develop Clear, Short-Term Goals

After you have worked through step 4 and made appropriate adjustments to your targeted roles, you should have a reasonable approximation of the path and key milestones required to attain that position from a long- and medium-term perspective. At this point, you should use that knowledge of the path and key milestones to develop clear and logical short-term goals that, if achieved, will put you on a path to attain your medium- and longer-term objectives.

By working from your end point backward, this should help to put your immediate objectives into a different perspective, resulting in short-term goals that are much better aligned with your longer-term objectives. This is very important; it is often difficult to change course without significant sacrifice—even early in a career—if you have started along a path that diverges from your overall objective—particularly if you want to change industries—since your experience even after a few years is typically valued much higher. Thus, ensuring that your work or efforts, even if you are still in school, are in alignment with your long-term objectives is crucial to establishing the foundation for future success.

To capitalize on the career mapping work you have completed (steps 1 through 4) and to develop specific short-term goals (step 5), you will want to assess where you are in terms of your current situation and its alignment with the overall plan. Consider whether you are currently on a clear path to attain your medium- and longer-term goals. (*Note*—it is absolutely critical that you be completely honest with yourself in order to ensure success.)

If you are still in school, you will want to assess not just the courses you have taken and the grades you have received but also whether you have developed the appropriate networks, resume, and ultimately have a clear path to a starting job in an industry and company with a career path that can help you attain, at minimum, your medium-term objectives. Your short-term objectives should address all of these aspects, with a heavy focus on those factors that will culminate in a job offer that will provide you with the opportunities to achieve your career goals. While in school, don't lose sight of the end-point objective, which is not only what classes you have taken and the grades that you received. Rather, these are just the enablers to your longer-term career plan. It will be very important to keep this in perspective when making choices about how best to balance and allocate your limited time between coursework, network development, internships, co-ops or other job experience opportunities, interview preparation (resume development, company research, etc.), and actual interviewing.

If you have already started your career, the same advice applies, but just in a different context. Start by assessing where you are relative to your medium- and longer-term goals. (Again, you need to be perfectly honest with yourself to make this truly worthwhile.) In assessing where you are currently relative to your medium- and longer-term goals, consider the industry you are in, your career progress and rate of ascent at your present employer. Part of the assessment process should involve considering whether there are continued or future career growth opportunities at a rate commensurate with achieving your longer-term goals in your current industry and with this specific employer. Realize that historical growth rates are not indicative of future growth, and that the skills, attributes, and approaches you use to achieve initial successes may not be the same as those needed to progress to higher levels in an organization. In setting your short-term goals, consider setting objectives that are not just specific desired jobs but also skills, networks, and other attributes necessary to continue to progress forward with your career. Keep the goals specific and measurable as much as possible.

Step 6: Develop a Periodic Milestone, Check-In Process

Whether you are in school or into your career, it is important that you periodically (probably every six months or so) assess where you are versus your objectives, particularly the specific short-term, tactical goals. This will give you an opportunity to adjust plans quickly and provide you with the best chance of achieving your longer-term targets.

Defining clear career goals and milestones, along with a periodic assessment and adjustment process, should significantly increase the efficiency and effectiveness of your time and provide perspective on those experiences, attributes, and skills required to achieve your maximum desired career potential.

Chapter 3
Building a Network

Building a strong network of contacts that you actively cultivate, grow, and maintain is important even early in your career. While it is rare that you can attain your highest career aspirations solely based on whom you know, a strong network of contacts who respect your skills, capabilities, and leadership attributes may provide you with valuable opportunities for career growth, ranging from future job opportunities to career benchmarking.

Developing a strong network takes time and can be more of an art than a science. However, there are some rules to consider as you begin this process. I recommend starting by considering what you are ultimately attempting to achieve from a career standpoint (reference the career targets you identified from chapter 2: "Goal Setting and Management"). Think about what types of people could help you to attain the opportunities, experiences, skills, attributes, leadership qualities, or other factors you need to progress along your desired career path. Recognize that this network will likely need to evolve over time and that those individuals who might be able to help you early in your career may very well be different from those who will help you get to higher levels along your desired career path.

Take advantage of the relationships that you already have developed with individuals who might be able to help you at different levels throughout your career path. If you are in school, this might mean professors who have strong connections in an industry or companies that align with your goals. It could also mean former classmates who have started their careers and appear to

29

be progressing fairly rapidly in an industry or company in which you have interest. You should also consider current classmates whom you respect and share similar career aspirations. Although these individuals might not have the influence to impact your career currently, they might be able to help you in the future. These current classmates may also provide you with good career benchmarks against which you can compare your progress over time in terms of experiences, opportunities, compensation, and overall career progression. Having reliable, external benchmarks, which you can obtain from peers working elsewhere, will be important throughout your career to provide outside perspective on these factors. (If you have already started your working career, LinkedIn.com provides a great medium for maintaining professional relationships, as well as tracking down former classmates or colleagues.)

If you are in the workforce, I also highly recommend identifying individuals at your employer who are in your functional discipline and are ahead of you in terms of level and already on a rapid career trajectory. Building strong professional relationships with other individuals on a "fast track" will not only provide you with a good resource for potential career guidance and mentoring, but may also give you access to new job opportunities sooner, or may simply provide increased exposure of your skills and capabilities to senior leadership who you would otherwise not yet have access to early in your career.

Developing a strong professional network with other respected and currently or potentially influential individuals will often take time and requires repeated exposure and consistently favorable impressions. The most valuable contacts will generally result from direct working relationships where you have been given the opportunity to demonstrate your leadership, vision, analytical abilities, creativity, work ethic, or other attributes in a highly compelling manner. Gaining confidence and trust in your abilities is critical for developing contacts who might provide you future job opportunities, projects or work that gives you accelerated exposure to senior leadership. When you are provided with an opportunity through a contact, it is very important that you meet and ideally exceed the expectations of these customers and your contact in order to capitalize on the opportunity. This will not only strengthen the relationship with your contact by making him or her look good, but will also increase the likelihood of receiving future opportunities from this contact. Further, it might provide the opportunity to develop other key contacts and build credibility and a reputation for strong work—all of which should help to advance your career at an accelerated pace.

Maintaining relationships with contacts can sometimes become difficult, particularly if individuals work at different companies or locations and as job responsibilities become increasingly greater and time-intensive. Recognize that career interests and priorities change over time with individuals, so it is natural that your network of contacts will evolve. For contacts that you don't interact with on a regular basis, I recommend establishing periodic check-ins to ensure that you maintain the relationship. I have found professional networking websites such as LinkedIn.com to be somewhat useful for this. This has also made reconnecting with old contacts less awkward—particularly if significant time has elapsed since you last interacted with them.

My network of contacts has been extremely helpful to me over the course of my career. Many of the initial contacts that I made while in school have been good resources to benchmark career progress in terms of responsibilities, opportunities afforded by their employers, and compensation. Other contacts that I developed early in my working career have been helpful in similar ways and have also led to consulting opportunities. Further, some of these contacts have resulted in my gaining job opportunities and leadership exposure that I don't believe I would have otherwise received.

One of the most trusted contacts in my network is an individual I met on my first day of full-time employment. Despite the fact that we both have switched companies several times since then, we have kept in close contact. This relationship has benefited both of us; we have a respected peer (i.e., each other) to confidentially discuss different potential career moves (both at our current employers and new ones) with consideration for job fit and likelihood of success, as well as the importance of potential moves to longer-range career goals; the implications of future roles; as well as the appropriateness of current and expected future compensation. As a result, both of us have made better, more thoughtful career decisions that have ensured career ascension in line with our individual career objectives.

As you begin to develop a strong network of contacts who respect your professional skills and capabilities, you will increase your likelihood of gaining exposure to projects, work, individuals, and ultimately new and higher-level job opportunities at an accelerated pace. Therefore, the sooner you can begin to build your network of professional contacts, the better.

Chapter 4
Internships

Whether you are an undergrad or graduate student, attaining an internship at a recognizable company and desirable work experience is probably the most important single step to procuring interviews for long-term employment at a company that will provide upward career mobility. In general, paid internships are actually more difficult to secure than full-time employment—there are simply fewer opportunities—since many companies do not have paid internship programs. Particularly in difficult economic times, paid internship opportunities can be fairly scarce. As a result, individuals who have earned the opportunity to work as paid interns are likely to separate themselves significantly from others in their desired field of work—especially if their work as interns is deemed valuable by potential future employers.

All else being equal, when it comes to internships, it is my opinion that the more recognizable the company name, the better (assuming the company is in good financial standing and has a reputation for being ethical). A known and respected company name on your resume will generally receive the attention of other prospective full-time employers. However, in order to make the internship experience really appealing to potential future employers, the work should also have strong perceived value. It is important that *you* find a way to provide your internship employer with work that is valued—even during the short time that you are employed. (Notice that I said it will be important that "you

33

provide" work that is valued, not that you are "provided with" work that will be valued.) Ideally, you will know before you start an internship what the work is that you will be doing for a company so that you can determine whether or not you want to accept the opportunity. Unfortunately, it is fairly common for specific work assignments not to be known or communicated prior to employment when it comes to internships. My advice would be to keep the end in mind—which, during the internship process, should be to ensure that you have good examples that illustrate how you added value for the company where you interned, and which could be reapplied at this company or a different company of your preference for full-time employment; important points when it comes time to build your resume and begin interviewing. Along these lines, if you find that the work being requested at your internship is *not* likely to be compelling to other potential employers, think about how you can increase the scope of your work to add additional value. In this case, don't ask for permission—just do it. You will almost certainly find that this not only creates a favorable impression with your employer, but will ensure that you will have something unique and considerably more impressive to discuss during future interviews.

In my case, I found that landing an internship was very challenging. While I had relatively good grades and some work experience (though the work experience was not particularly relevant to my major), even getting an interview for an internship was difficult. (With this being my junior year, I recognized that this was likely the last opportunity for an internship prior to graduation.) As a result, I had to become more creative and worked to proactively leverage the experiences that I had in a more compelling manner. (For those of you who have been

34

reading from the beginning of this book, you will recall the example where I was able to take my knowledge from working in the summers at the School of Agriculture to assemble a database on what I believed would be good predictors of crop yields. From there, I utilized statistical modeling techniques learned in a statistics class to develop an algorithm that effectively predicted crop yields based on this environmental data.) While I was not having success gaining interest from desired employees in internship opportunities, I decided to see whether I might have more success within an academic setting. To test this, I contacted a professor in the School of Horticulture and shared the output of the predictive statical model for crop yields that I had developed. Ultimately, this gained enough interest to earn an internship in the Horticulture Department, despite having a nontraditional major (finance) for this type of work.

Receiving this internship provided me with experiences that—although not perfectly applicable to my desired career in corporate finance—provided technical credibility and highlighted my creativity and motivation. At this point, I had a difficult decision to make. It was my senior year, and I could push myself to take additional credits to graduate, knowing that I had completed an internship with reasonable experiences but without a recognizable company name or specific finance application. The alternative was to stay in school for an additional semester, which would provide me with the opportunity to hopefully get a stronger internship in the following summer, and also allow me to add a second major in real estate, which I believed would help me to further expand my applied financial analysis skills. Ultimately, I believed that the benefits potentially provided by gaining a more recognizable internship were going to be very important to receiving a full-time opportunity consistent with my career aspirations—so I elected to stay in school for an additional semester and began to search for stronger, more relevant internship opportunities.

It became very clear early in the interview process in the following spring that I had made a good decision to pursue the agricultural statistics internship and ultimately stay in school for an additional semester in order to seek out a more applicable and recognizable internship. Unlike previous years, I received several interviews for internship opportunities, and my work in the Horticulture Department provided me with concrete examples of work that highlighted my technical skills in a way that, although not perfectly applicable to finance, was fairly compelling. Ultimately, I received an offer for a finance internship with a very large and familiar consumer products company, which I accepted.

This internship provided me with the opportunity to work for an extremely recognizable and respected company. It also afforded me the opportunity to work on a high-profile project where I was able to learn significantly and build my resume in the process. As an intern at this company, performance expectations were high, with projects being real business cases and issues that needed solutions. My project involved leading the development of a competitive profitability analysis for a newly acquired portion of their business where information was still not fully understood.

This project required me to work closely with the brand management and market research teams to understand competitive product offerings, volumes/market share, and pricing. I also worked closely with the research organization to understand the key product attributes and differences between competitive products that were likely to influence material cost. Finally, I worked with the engineering organization to attempt to understand differences in manufacturing costs. To pull this information together and provide the ability to change competitive assumptions as new and better information was acquired, I developed a comprehensive, interactive model that allowed the competitive analysis to be easily updated after my internship was completed and I returned to school. (The addition of interactive update capabilities was a feature that was not requested, but an extra step that I included to enhance the project's value—something that was clearly recognized by my manager and other influential leaders at the conclusion of my work.)

I was fortunate to get an opportunity from this company and I made the most of it. I worked long days and many weekends to make sure that I could meet the lofty demands of my internal customers and ultimately exceed them on some aspects, such as the development of the interactive model that provided for easy updates and a refreshable, ongoing competitive assessment, rather than simply a one-time analysis. As a result of this experience, I was able to make some impressive updates to my resume that significantly separated me from virtually all of my peers who were also looking for interviews for full-time employment in corporate finance. (I also had an offer from this company to return for full-time employment, which was a nice perk from a successful internship as well.) Further, as I received interviews (which was not a problem after this internship—in fact, I probably turned down as many interviews as I accepted), I had extremely compelling and tangible examples of work experiences that were easily understood by potential future employers.

Using my example, I would strongly encourage you to take the process of obtaining a quality internship very seriously—even if it means changing your graduation plans (as I did) or making other sacrifices. If you do not land an internship with a company that has name recognition or will provide you with the quality of work that you believe will effectively build your resume or provide you with compelling work examples during full-time employment interviews, then you may need to get creative (in fact, this is probably the norm rather than the exception). This might mean taking an additional semester to graduate to allow for an extra summer to find a strong internship to augment your resume. Ultimately, the additional semester might not only allow you to add additional courses that will help you in your career or lighten your course load, but also allow you to dedicate more time to those "core" courses (as described in chapter 1: "Maximizing Your Education") that will provide significant value in your profession after graduation.

Finally, do not forget that *you* control how much time you invest in your internship, regardless of the employer or the work that is required. If the work requested by your internship employer will not add to your resume or provide compelling examples to share in interviews, then you will want to think about how you can creatively improve the situation. Consider opportunities where you could provide additional value for the employer. Most employers will be excited to see the initiative and will welcome additional value-adding work that is self-started.

Chapter 5
Selecting a Company

Choosing the right companies with which to interview is a difficult but critical task. It is natural to default to companies that: are perceived as high-tech, have products or services in a particular area of interest, have family or friends who work there, provide higher initial compensation, are located in a geographically preferred area, or are presently courting you because you previously worked or interned there.

While all these factors are important, I would strongly recommend that you consider some of the criteria outlined for internships for company name recognition and reputation, as well as the type of work that you will be doing, and whether it will be recognized and valued outside of the specific employer. Then I would add one more crucial factor in considering full-time employment—career progression opportunities.

Like it or not, company name and reputation can have a significant impact on the perceptions of you by other potential employers. While working for a company perceived as respectable and having talented employees does not guarantee an interview or job offer, it will often help a candidate to stand out—particularly if a firm has experience with bringing in strong employees with previous experience at that employer. Therefore, when all else is equal, I would recommend looking at larger companies with positive name recognition—it might provide you a "halo effect" benefit if you ever choose to change employers. (This is particularly relevant for your initial employer, as it creates the foundation for all future moves.)

Understanding the work you would be doing at a prospective employer and the potential career path is even more important in selecting a company than company name recognition. However, company reputation is clearly an overriding factor in some extreme cases. Unfortunately, gaining a deep understanding of likely work assignments or specific career progression opportunities might be difficult to discern before you submit your resume for consideration. These factors should become your top criteria for selecting a job after you have completed the interviewing process. Therefore, it is useful to do due diligence to screen potential employers before the time-consuming interviewing process. (More specific guidance about assessing potential job assignments and company career progression opportunities will be discussed in chapter 8: "Selecting a Job.")

Chapter 6
Getting an Interview
(Developing and Distributing Your Resume)

Getting an interview is often a function of having a good resume. However, you first have to get your resume into the hands of employers who are interested in your resume. I will discuss both aspects in this chapter and give examples of how to develop a compelling resume and get it in the right hands of potential employers using various methods.

Building a Compelling Resume

For individuals who are still in school and have little or no full-time work experience, earning a respectable grade point average (at least 3.3 on a 4.0 scale) from a recognized school is the first part of building a strong resume. If your grade point average in your major is significantly stronger than your overall GPA, then it is advisable to highlight this on your resume. Some employers have minimum thresholds for new-hire grade point averages. However, whether you have a 3.5 or a 4.0 generally will not have significant bearing on your likelihood of receiving an interview. As discussed in chapter 4, having an impressive internship is probably the most important factor (assuming you have a reasonably respectable GPA) that you can have to differentiate yourself from other potential candidates.

Prior to an interview, your resume is the only mechanism you have to share who you are and what you can bring to a potential employer. Therefore, you will want to make it incredibly compelling. It goes without saying that spelling and grammar should be flawless. This includes maintaining consistency in voice as well as format and punctuation.

You must be able to effectively convey the work you have done at internships and previous jobs within your resume. You want the readers of your resume to have enough information on what you have done to be able to assess whether you might be a potential fit with their company. Thus, describe the work that you have done concisely and in a way that generates interest. For each employment example (whether it be part-time, full-time, or internship), I recommend including a statement about your role and responsibilities to provide some background on the nature of your work. With this as a base, provide summary bullets on key projects, activities, or accomplishments. Within these bullets, *be sure to highlight the specific actions you took and the result of these actions or accomplishments from your work*. A resume is not the place to be bashful—highlight the work you have done and the results that you have delivered!

If you do not have examples that you believe will cause you to stand out from other candidates, my advice is to think through how you can change this—starting with the courses you are taking or the company where you are currently working. As discussed in chapters 1 and 4, there are usually great opportunities in your school or work projects to take the work above and beyond traditional expectations—even if this is not something that is being requested as part of the assignment. These are perfect opportunities to proactively create work products that will be noticed by anyone reviewing your resume—particularly if one of your professors or colleagues is willing to provide a reference for you to validate the quality of this effort and that augments your resume.

I do have one caution on resumes: exclude descriptions that might be considered confidential in nature by current or prior employers. Generally, it is good to exclude anything that references financial or operational performance figures, including but not limited to: volumes, sales, pricing, market share, growth rates, profitability, or production capacity. If you have examples of performance impacts, talk in terms of percentages (e.g., improved profitability by 10 percent versus budget, reduced spending by 3 percent versus prior year, etc.). This can help to provide context around the impact of your work without sharing anything that your current or prior employer may find confidential.

Getting Your Resume in Front of Potential Employers

Once your resume is completed, you will need to get it in the hands of potential employers in order to get an interview. If you are currently enrolled at a reasonably large college or university, your particular school may have a career placement office. In the best-case scenario, employers may actually come directly to your school to interview candidates, selecting resumes from a school database, and asking students to interview. However, if you are not currently enrolled in school or are attending a school that does not include this service, then you will need to employ different options, such as directly contacting companies, job boards, or using external recruiting agencies.

Contacting companies directly regarding potential job openings is easier now than ever. Most medium- to large-sized companies have a careers section on their websites, with many showing currently available positions for external candidates, often by function, level, and location. You might have specific companies in mind that you want to contact directly through their websites. If you are just starting your company contact list, Fortune magazine provides a listing of the five hundred largest publicly traded companies (based on net sales); this may be a good resource for quickly identifying companies to contact that could be a good fit with your career objectives. The drawback to contacting companies directly is that this process can sometimes be fairly time-consuming, depending on the complexity and nature of submitting information. It may also be difficult to know how long the job has been posted, where employers are in their search processes, and when to expect to hear back from them should they be interested in your resume and interviewing you.

It is increasingly common for companies to post jobs externally on job websites in addition to their own websites. (Monster.com, Careerbuilder.com, theLadders.com, and 6figurejobs.com are all commonly used.) Many of these websites allow users to view multiple job openings, along with the company's job qualifications and applicants' expected and required experience. Applying for jobs via the many job websites is often less time-consuming than directly contacting individual companies because they request more standard formats for information needed of applicants.

Some companies handle all of their hiring needs through internal corporate resources (either by function, region, or centrally through human resources). Other companies may use a combination of internal and external recruiting resources to identify new employees. Therefore, if you receive a response to a job application, it is possible that you might be contacted directly by the employer or by an externally selected recruiting agent. In either case, it is likely that before being asked to do an onsite interview, you will be asked to do one or more phone interviews before the company will invest resources to bring you onsite, particularly if you are not local.

If you apply to a position via one of the many independent job sites (e.g., Monster.com, Careerbuilder.com, etc.), you will most likely be contacted by a recruiting agency representative. From there, it is likely that the recruiter might have other jobs that could be a potential fit that they want to discuss with you. In some situations, recruiters might have knowledge of job openings that are simply not available on the normal job sites or company websites. They also might be aware of openings before their posting. Therefore, recruiters can be a very valuable resource in your job search.

In addition to making contact with independent recruiters through job sites, you might want to contact these recruiting firms directly. Internet searches for "recruiters" based on functional specialty or geographical location or by looking at who is hosting multiple positions in your area of interest is a good starting point. (You can also reach out to colleagues within your network—as described in chapter 3: "Building a Network"—who might have had a good experience using a particular set of recruiters or recruitment firms.) Particularly if you have work experience, having a LinkedIn.com profile that is current will often result in recruiters contacting you directly for roles that match-up with your experience. In fact, LinkedIn is becoming increasingly popular as a tool used by companies and external recruiting agencies to identify potential job candidates—so make sure that you have an account and that you keep it updated. There are also several resume "distribution" services, such as resumezapper.com, that can be effective at passing your resume to numerous independent recruiters (for a fee) based on geographic, industry, or other preferences. It is likely that recruiters who receive your resume will make direct contact with you via phone or e-mail quickly if they are working with companies that have jobs that they believe are a good fit with the qualifications on your resume. Using independent recruiters often accelerates your job search, and they are typically free of charge to potential employees, as most recruiters are compensated by employers when they identify a candidate who is ultimately hired.

There are a lot of advantages to using recruiters in your job search—particularly if you are already in the workforce and do not have a school placement office to help with your search. However, it is important to be aware of the financial arrangement between corporations and independent recruiters as you are working through your job search process. While most independent recruiters are interested in finding you a good opportunity, they are also interested in getting paid—which only happens when an individual accepts a new job offer. Before accepting a position with a new employer, you will want to make certain that *you* have enough information to feel comfortable that this company will provide you with the opportunities to grow your career at your desired pace. My advice: don't take a job based on a recruiter being comfortable—take the job only when *you* are completely comfortable. (More specific guidance on assessing potential job assignments and company career progression opportunities will be discussed in chapter 8: "Selecting a Job.")

Chapter 7
Interviewing

All the work you have done to build a strong resume through coursework and examinations that culminate in a grade point average, along with internships and other work experience, all come together at the time of the interview. Your resume and its distribution to potential employers simply got you in the door with the employer. At the interview, expect that you will have to substantiate your resume, proving the competency level implied by your grades and expanding on your work experiences in a compelling manner. Remember, you are trying to convince this company that you are the best candidate for the job, recognizing that there are other qualified candidates available now or in the near future. So, you will need to deliver a highly persuasive message during your limited time with the prospective employer and each of the interviewers.

I recommend preparing for an interview in a manner similar to preparing for a final examination or highly important presentation, with four critical steps to the preparation, as follows: 1) really know your resume; 2) research the company where you are interviewing; 3) prepare answers for questions you may be asked; and 4) bring highly compelling, non-confidential examples to clearly illustrate the quality of your work—in a tangible manner, if possible.

Step 1: Really Know Your Resume

Really knowing your resume means much more than being able to recite your grade point average or even the key bullets next to your work or internship experience. To be truly prepared for an interview, you should know your resume from every aspect imaginable. Consider the questions that an interviewer might like to know about your coursework or projects you have highlighted from work or internship experience. Be prepared so that if questioned, you can briefly but succinctly provide a bit of context about any element of your resume, along with clear examples of what you did (that are ideally unique) to help deliver a clear and compelling, positive result.

You should also be prepared to give an enthusiastic two- to three-minute overview of your background, touching on those key points in your resume that the specific employer with whom you are interviewing is interested. (Make sure to know your audience—what is important to one company may not be relevant to all; tailor your message to fit the expected interests of the specific company and interviewers, and if possible—consider what each specific interviewer really wants to know about you when preparing for your interview.) Many interviews start with the interviewer asking the candidate to provide a bit of background on themselves and their resumes. Having a rehearsed and memorized summary of your background, key accomplishments, and particular interest in the specific company and job opportunity should be a top priority.

Step 2: Research the Company before Your Interview

Company websites often provide virtually everything you need, from product and service summaries, to company size, locations, vision, and financial performance, as well as projections. Familiarize yourself with this information, taking notes and committing important information to memory prior to your interview. Most interviewers will want to understand your particular interest in their company. Having knowledge about the company will highlight your initiative outside of simply showing up for the interview. It will also help to confirm your desire to work for the company. During your company research, make notes of appropriate questions to ask the interviewer—most interviewers will leave some time for candidate questions about the company and the particular job. If you are given the time to ask questions, consider this as an opportunity for you to get answers to questions you have about the job, company, career path beyond the open job, etc. Perhaps as important—this is an opportunity for you to ask insightful questions (based on your company research) that will further highlight your ability to think, reason, analyze, and synthesize information. One of the biggest mistakes that you can make is to *not* have a series of good questions for each interviewer—as this will be interpreted by many interviewers as either a lack of interest, preparation, or insights. Below is a list of potential questions that should provide you with additional perspective around the specific position, the company, and career progression opportunities.

> *1). What skills or attributes do you find are most important to success in this role? Are these skills or attributes the same as are generally needed for success within other roles at this company?*

50

2). What is the biggest challenge that an individual will face coming into this particular role?

3). What do you like most about this company?
4). What do you see as the biggest challenges to this company—competitive, or other?
5). What types of future opportunities would exist after this role in terms of career progression?

Asking some or all of these questions will help to highlight your interest to the interviewer and also provide you with better insight into the job and company to determine whether this is somewhere that would provide the career progression opportunities that you desire. Notice that there are no questions around compensation, benefits, vacation, flexible work schedules, etc. While these are questions that you will certainly want answers to, you will want to save them until you have an offer and can discuss them with the hiring manager or recruiter. (The exception to this is if you are working directly with a recruiter. If a recruiter contacts you about a role it is beneficial to both you and the recruiter to be transparent very early in your discussion around expectations—particularly as it relates to compensation, location, and other job or company attribute requirements.)

The opportunity to ask questions of employees within a company is a really great way to get answers to questions that you just can't find through external resources. Consider any outstanding questions that you may have had when you were deciding whether to consider targeting this company (per chapter 5: "Selecting a Company"), and if appropriate try to get answers to your questions. One final thought—it is completely appropriate to ask the same questions of different interviewers within the same company, particularly if they involve a person's opinion—as this can provide a different perspective based on each individual's experiences.

Step 3: Prepare Answers for Questions You Might Be Asked

This element of interview preparation involves creating a list of the questions that you expect to be asked in your interview. Start by carefully considering questions that might logically be raised about your resume (as highlighted previously in this chapter), as well as questions that you expect a company to want to have answers to for a person applying for this particular job. Many of the questions that you assemble will probably apply fairly equally among different companies. However, make sure to consider the perspective of each potential employer and modify your question list as appropriate, based on the lens of each particular organization. Typical questions that you can expect might include the following:

- *Why do you have interest in working for this company?*
- *Tell me about yourself.*
- *Could you walk me through the highlights of your resume?*
- *How did you decide to select your particular college or university?*
- *Why did you choose to major in your field of study?*

- What is your greatest accomplishment? Why do you consider this your greatest accomplishment?
- What are your three greatest strengths?
- What is your biggest weakness or opportunity? What are you doing to address this?
- Tell me about a time where someone was not pleased with your work. What happened? Why?
- Tell me about a time where you missed a deadline—how did you handle this?
- Give me an example of a recommendation for improvement that you self-initiated. What was the outcome or result?
- What are your career goals? What is your ultimate target position?
- How would others describe you?
- Can you give me an example of how you have worked with other individuals with very different ideas or perspectives to achieve a common goal? Why were you successful?
- Have you ever been put in a position where you had an ethical dilemma? How did you handle this?
- Can you provide an example of where one of your superiors was not thinking about something correctly? Were you able to change his or her mind? How did you achieve this?
- How have you or would you manage underperforming employees?
- What are your criteria for assessing employee talent?

- *Why should I hire you to work for this company?*
- *What are your unique attributes and how will they make you effective in this job?*
- *Have you managed people or teams previously? What techniques have you found to be most successful?*
- *What approach do you use to develop other employees? Can you give me some examples of where this has worked in the past?*

This is by no means a comprehensive list of questions. In fact, it is likely that in any given interview, you will be faced with at least one question that you were not prepared to answer—most likely more. In this situation, carefully consider what the interviewer is trying to determine. In some cases, you might find that one of your well-rehearsed answers will actually apply nicely to the particular question being asked. If appropriate, you might find that using one of these answers effectively answers the question. However, always be certain to answer the specific question being asked. Not having an answer to a question is never a good option. For any questions that you were not prepared to answer, be sure to add it to your list of interview questions at the conclusion of the interview so that you can prepare a thoughtful response if you get the same or similar question in a future interview.

During an interview or in preparing for an interview, think carefully about why a question is asked and what the interviewer is trying to determine with an answer. It is very common for interviewers to ask a candidate to provide "specific examples" of work previously completed or leadership behaviors demonstrated when answering questions. This style of questioning is generally referred to as "targeted selection" or "behavioral interviewing". If asked to provide an example, be sure to provide a very specific example—don't speak in general or hypothetical terms (this is a very common problem for many individuals—both inexperienced and experienced candidates). In considering the answer to your question, make sure to provide some background for the interviewer, who will not likely be familiar with the details of your particular experience. Start by providing some perspective about the role that you had and then the specific action that you took. Finally, explain the outcome of the work that you did. *You will want to provide examples that credibly illustrate your ability to effectively deliver positive results. Being able to articulate complex answers and examples in a creative, intuitive manner is critical.* Remember this with the examples that you choose and your method for delivering your communication to the interviewer.

It is very common—particularly in on-site corporate interviews where you might meet with several different interviewers—to receive the same interview question (or a similar iteration) on more than one occasion. While you do not need to have a different example for each interviewer, you should consider this when developing answers to common questions. Try to have some variety in the examples you choose to answer similar questions. This will highlight your breadth of experience and knowledge and also ensure that you have an appropriate answer for the question being asked, based on the context of the interview and the experiences of the interviewer.

Step 4: Developing Highly Compelling Examples

The final aspect of the interview preparation process that I recommend to maximize the effectiveness of the interview involves developing example materials to take with you (and potentially leave behind) for interviews. This is a rarely used but often highly effective technique that provides greater context for illustrating examples of projects or work that you have completed and want to share during an interview.

I effectively started using this technique while in school looking for internships and have continued to use this practice in interviews ever since. In fact, it was my presentation of the previously mentioned project about forecasting crop yields using a database of key environmental data that ultimately led to gaining my first internship in the School of Agriculture at the University of Wisconsin. I continued to reuse this project, as well as another school project, when looking for other internship, and ultimately, full-time job opportunities. For interviewing, I would bring with me a hard copy of the reports to share with interviewers if appropriate. On more than one occasion interviewers wanted to take a copy to review following the interview. In addition to providing some helpful context and validation to examples, this technique caused me to stand-out from other potential candidates.

As another example, when I decided to leave my job at the financial software start-up company, I needed to be able to provide some compelling examples of my work—as my ability to garner valuable references from this experience was somewhat limited, and the company name was not very recognizable. However, I had some very compelling work experiences that I wanted to share, albeit potentially fantastic, but without a tangible way of illustrating them. One of my major roles at the software company was to develop a sophisticated prototype version of the software utilizing Excel and Visual Basic. However, I knew that starting up a computer during an interview to showcase an example of this would not be practical, given time limitations, and would have realistically been a bit clumsy, even if I could. In trying to determine how to showcase the efforts and results that I had invested in this software development, what I had forgotten was that I also wrote the 140-page user manual to accompany it, which included screen shots and examples to illustrate the power of the software and my contributions. Ultimately, I decided to bring a bound copy of this with me to interviews and was able to reference it in conjunction with any examples of work while I was with the software firm. This technique proved to be very effective, enabling me to engage and impress interviewers with my work on a dimension that could not be as effectively conveyed through a resume or words during an interview. Ultimately, I was able to turn a potential weak spot on my resume into one of my strongest, most compelling examples of vision, creativity, and work ethic.

If you choose to utilize this powerful technique, just be sure to limit what you share to information that is not considered confidential by your current or prior employers. If you are utilizing previous school projects, this may not be an issue. However, if you hope to share projects from a company where you worked, then you should definitely remove anything that would identify the company or its brands. Further, if there is anything that would be considered confidential by current or previous employers, this information should be excluded or replaced by examples that illustrate concepts that you want to share without disclosing confidential information.

Wardrobe Considerations

One last item on interviews—dress for success. While there are plenty of opinions on what to wear to an interview and its impacts, I actually believe that there is really only one consideration—make yourself look presentable enough so as not to draw attention to your wardrobe. Ideally, the interview should stay focused on your accomplishments and determination of whether and how you will be able to help the company if and when you are offered a job. Based on my experiences of interviewing and being interviewed, I truly believe that your wardrobe choices for an interview cannot help you but clearly can hurt you. Choose a wardrobe that presents you well and consider that this is one last indication to your potential, future employer about your level of seriousness about them and the interview, as well as your attention to detail. Like the four techniques described earlier in this chapter about preparing to present yourself to interviewers, think about your wardrobe in the same context. Determine what outfits present you best. Then, ensure that whatever you wear is consistent or one step above the wardrobe worn by executives at the company where you are interviewing. In general, you are better to overdress for the interview, but don't completely overdo it.

If you are working or going to school full-time, you might find it difficult to dedicate the time to do the preparation that I have recommended in this chapter. However, don't forget what the point of all of your previous work was designed to do—particularly if you are in school. Ultimately, your schoolwork is a means to help provide you with the tools to get a job and establish a career path that is consistent with your own, long-term personal goals. Therefore, I highly encourage you to invest the time to *seriously* prepare for interviews with any companies where you have a genuine interest in working. If you are willing to make this time investment to thoroughly prepare using the four interviewing fundamentals described in this chapter, then I am confident that you will find the success rate from your interviews, in terms of job offers, to be very high.

Chapter 8
Selecting a Job

Effectively selecting a job is an essential element in building the foundation for a strong career that has timely advancement opportunities aligned with your defined goals. Each job you choose has a direct impact on the work you do, the experiences you gain, the exposure you get, and possible sponsorship. Each job also impacts the network you develop, your resume, and ultimately, your perceived internal and external value, which will generally translate into compensation and consideration for future advancement opportunities. The point is that the jobs you select will have a major bearing on your career path and all of the other elements that influence it, so thinking through your choices and decisions is very important.

Recall that chapter 5: "Selecting a Company," discussed how crucial it is to target companies that ideally provide name recognition, a strong reputation, and most of all, the opportunity for career advancement. In the initial stages of selecting a company, it is often difficult to ascertain all the information necessary to determine whether a company might provide the optimal opportunities to attain your career goals. In some companies, particularly larger conglomerates, your ability to maximize success is more a function of the role or job where you start than the overall company. (To elaborate on this, let me share a personal example. When I was interviewing for full-time opportunities prior to graduation from college, I had one company that made me an offer for a role that was in distribution analysis rather than my desired focus area of finance. Essentially, the company was trying to bring in individuals with stronger analytical skills and decided that a finance background would provide this. While this was a reputable company, it was totally unclear whether this role would help me to move into their finance group or if I would be headed down a path that was not aligned with my career objectives. I ultimately decided to pass on this job opportunity.) It is, therefore, necessary to understand the role for which you are interviewing before you accept a job, regardless of company name or reputation.

This chapter explores the criteria for selecting a job, as well as techniques for gathering additional information to help you make the most informed decision. To ensure that a job you're selecting aligns with your long-term career goals, there are four major questions that you should consider and attempt to answer, as follows: 1) What are the responsibilities and expectations of your initial role? 2) Beyond the initial role for which you are interviewing, what career path opportunities exist? 3) Does this career path provide long-term flexibility? 4) Will your compensation be aligned with your responsibilities and personal goals?

Question 1: What are the Responsibilities and Expectations of Your Initial Role?

Understanding the responsibilities of a new role is critical to ensure that it aligns with your career goals. Make sure your expectations are reasonable, particularly if this is your first job. For example—and despite your desires—it is unlikely that you will be redefining the corporate strategy

61

for a large corporation immediately upon college graduation. However—as with each of the other four factors in considering a new job—you will want to ensure your new job passes the "external validation test"; that is, the work that you are doing (or at least a significant aspect of it) should provide you with skills and knowledge that you can apply outside the company you are considering, and ultimately provide you with valuable examples for your resume. If you expect that the work for a particular job will not be perceived as valuable by other future employers, then it is probably not something that you will want to pursue. With this said, recognize that with many jobs, *the value is in what you make of it.*

When assessing a new role within a company, I highly recommend some due diligence to determine the "condition of the desk"; in other words, you will want to understand why there is a vacancy and whether you will have an overlap with the individual leaving the position. Filling a vacated job—in particular, if someone has left the company—can be highly challenging, especially when coming into the role from school or a different company. As much as possible, you want to make sure that the job you are going to fill will set you up for success and recognition. This is generally within your control, but external factors might have an impact, so be sure to consider them.

Whenever possible, assess your prospective manager or supervisor to determine whether you believe that your styles, work approaches, and work ethics will be compatible. This will be particularly valuable for gaining support and sponsorship for further career progression in an organization, given that advancement is often heavily impacted by your performance and potential as assessed by your direct manager.

Question 2: Beyond the Initial Role for which you are interviewing, what Career Path Opportunities Exist?

Having a clear understanding of what career path opportunities exist beyond the initial role for which you are interviewing is very important. In large companies, career paths and levels are often clearly defined for each function. Your open desire to understand this before accepting an offer should not be a surprise to large prospective employers—in fact, they even expect it. Understanding the logical next roles in a career path with a company, along with responsibilities as well as expectations about length of time in different roles and typical requirements for promotions, are factors that should be considered. As you assess the role that you are contemplating from an external perspective, you should also think through likely subsequent roles in a career path with this company, making sure that the job responsibilities will provide you with career- and resume-building skills and experiences. To validate the legitimacy of the feedback you receive about the career opportunities beyond the initial role, it is often helpful to hear examples of other employees who have advanced from the role you are being considered for and understand where they are currently in the company. If possible, it can also be helpful to hear examples of senior leaders in your area of interest and understand whether any of them ever held the role for which you are interviewing, and what their subsequent career path entailed.

A useful technique for assessing potential career opportunities is to map out the typical career path from the role for which you are interviewing all the way through your ultimate target role. (This is similar to the exercise that you completed on career maps in chapter 2, but in this case, you should ideally be able to get your prospective employer to help you complete this.) Having a sense for the population of other employees at each level and the typical time they spent in the position will also be useful for understanding the general difficulty level you can expect in achieving your goals. This should also help to highlight potential "stall-out" or career "stagnation" points that you will want to be very mindful of if you select a role with a particular employer. Virtually any career path has some bottleneck points, but they will differ from one employer to another and might be impacted by the level of growth and human capital investment at a particular company. Recognizing the level and location of these bottlenecks might help you choose between employers. Advanced knowledge of this can also help you to set some specific "trigger" points, at which time you will want to seriously consider your long-term career prospects with a particular employer if your career is stagnating.

If you don't see a career path that interests you through at least one job beyond the one for which you are interviewing, then it is probably not a good career move to take that job with that particular employer. This matters because, from the standpoint of a career path, if you don't see upward mobility, when the time comes to switch companies, you will most likely only get a similar job with another company, rather than a higher-level role. I know several individuals who have fallen into this situation, which has led to a series of company changes without any significant career progression. This has ultimately resulted in career stagnation that probably could have been avoided with a more thoughtful selection of employers, based on career opportunities and likely expected job fit. Usually, it takes time to gain credibility and sponsorship, typically through consistently solid performance over time (this is especially true when switching to a new employer where your "track record" is not substantiated). So, make sure that you have the intention of sticking with a particular employer before making a move, if you want be able to take full advantage of the change.

One final point to consider as it relates to selecting a new role—most employers do not positively view frequent employer switching. (This further validates the aforementioned advice about thinking beyond the initial role and ensuring that you see at least one additional upward promotion at this employer.) The logic is that most employers are interested in hiring and investing in individuals for long-term retention. Frequent job changes on your resume do not generally instill confidence that your future will be different from your past. Therefore, carefully consider the long-term potential of a new opportunity before deciding to pursue it.

Question 3: Does this Career Path provide Long-Term Flexibility?

When thinking about a potential new role, you will want to consider the impacts of this decision on your future career flexibility. In addition to understanding the career ladder at a particular employer and your ability to progress there, you should also consider the ramifications of this decision from an external perspective (i.e., will the training and skills developed at this employer apply reasonably well at other companies?). Understanding the level of specialization required by your work at a new employer, as well as the size of the market where this company operates, will ensure there are other jobs at companies similar to the one you are considering. This may not matter if you are in the later part of your career. However, even if you initially believe that you have selected the "ideal" long-term employer, there is always the risk of the unexpected—such as corporate financial distress or downsizing—which might be outside of your control. Thus, it is generally wise to consider looking for a job that will provide you with tools that can be reapplied and valued at another company in the future. This provides flexibility if a better career opportunity arises externally, or if you need to find different employment due to external factors.

In addition to assessing the market size and the potential applicability of the specialized tools and skills you develop at one company, you should also consider the likely growth of the industry in which the company competes, the historical and expected growth of the prospective employer, and the potential for your career growth based on the opportunities and unique characteristics of the company. I should note that while the growth rates and trends in certain industries might not be incredibly strong, the sheer size of their markets can provide significant career opportunities. The same can be said for larger, more established companies. It is generally more difficult for larger corporations to achieve the same overall growth rates as smaller companies. However, it is common for opportunities for career growth in certain functions to be faster than that of the overall corporation; at least until senior management levels are reached. Identifying unique opportunities such as this might be difficult, but they can provide the potential for more rapid career growth if they are understood and factored into your decision making.

Another consideration, when assessing a potential new job and its career path implications, is to understand where this path ultimately leads for someone with high aspirations. In other words, you will want to gain a sense for what the most senior role is within this particular field, as well as the reporting relationships to this position. Depending on the aggressiveness of your career aspirations, this could be very relevant. Sometimes, this can be determined by assessing the C-level executive roles and the backgrounds of the individuals filling those roles. Other times, you might find that the highest-ranking person within this field might not even be in an executive position. Understanding where a career path peaks within a company and the levels of management (i.e., layers) between your potential role and the most senior role, should provide some perspective on future career opportunities afforded by a potential employer. For example, it is fairly standard for a company to have a chief marketing officer, chief financial officer, chief strategy officer, and chief technology officer, in addition to the chief executive officer. With each of these positions, reporting arrangements and career ladder relationships, down through entry level positions within those functional areas, is often fairly clear. However, someone starting a role in facilities management, customer service, or another functional area might find that the career ladder has very limited career mobility at a particular company, often bounded by that most senior position—assuming you would like to remain in that particular function.

Finally, in considering the flexibility that different potential employers afford a specific career path in a particular field, you should also carefully consider the responsibilities and expectations of a career in this field. Generally, roles that ultimately lead to the management of people, particularly highly skilled individuals who will also be considered for management positions themselves someday, will be valued more highly and compensated more generously. Recognize that each company might have its own unique approach and perspective on how to use and manage functional support. Therefore, understanding how a prospective employer handles this relative to industry norms will ensure you are providing yourself with the right experiences and responsibilities to maximize your long-term future career flexibility.

Question 4: Will Your Compensation be aligned with Your Responsibilities and Personal Goals?

Compensation is often a significant factor in selecting a job and a career. After all, most of us are working with the intention of making money, with more being better than less, all else being equal. However, in assessing jobs, there is often more to consider than just the starting salary. Recognize that different employers have independent perspectives and policies on compensation, ranging from starting pay scales to the timing and significance of raises to the level and degree of bonuses, or other variable pay incentives that are included in employee compensation. Corporate culture and expectations of employee availability and overall time investment also differ significantly between prospective employers. All of these factors should be understood to the degree possible and considered in your decision-making process when selecting a job.

Benchmarking compensation opportunities with career progression at different employers might be somewhat difficult beyond the initial role you are considering. However, you can often glean this information from thoughtful questions after you receive a job offer; it is generally expected that an individual will want to understand what potential long-term career opportunities exist when selecting a new employer, particularly for individuals with significant prior work experience. When benchmarking across companies, recognize that titles are almost never universal. Therefore, compare opportunities (both current and future) based on responsibility levels, required experience, organizational size, relationship to senior leadership, and other relevant factors.

Techniques for Gathering this Information

It can be difficult to gain the appropriate information to thoroughly assess potential jobs and longer-term career opportunities. However, there are several ways to effectively gather this information to make more-informed, better career decisions. As discussed earlier, before an interview, you will have limited ability to discern significant details about specific job responsibilities and their external applicability, or to understand longer-term career opportunities. However, in most interview situations (particularly on-site, multiple-person interviews), candidates will be given time to ask questions.

It is surprising to me how few questions candidates typically ask during job interviews. This is an ideal time to collect answers to many of the questions you might have about the specific job opportunity, as well as the career path within a company. I recommend asking any of these questions you might have if time allows in your interview. Questions about job responsibilities, key customers, exposure opportunities, reporting relationships (direct and indirect), expected assignment duration, why a position is vacant, and the typical career path are all appropriate. In addition to gathering critical feedback to help you in your employment decision, your questions have the added benefit of highlighting your level of engagement and interest in the company. However, use your judgment at the time of the interview in regards to which questions to ask, or prioritize them, given time constraints and an interviewer's desire or ability to answer them.

Prospective employers will often address additional questions after they extend an offer. It is common for the hiring manager or another representative (often from human resources) to contact individuals with job offers specifically to provide additional support about making a job decision. This provides another opportunity to get answers to questions you might not have asked or addressed sufficiently during the interviewing process. After an offer is extended, you will have more latitude to ask more detailed questions about compensation for the prospective role, as well as longer-term opportunities and expectations.

Regarding how much career flexibility is provided by a particular industry, employer, job, or career path, you will need to use your best judgment. Based on the knowledge that you have gained from your questions, consider the degree the work you would do at this employer would be valued at other organizations. Try to assess the size of the market or industry and the likely demand for similar roles outside the particular company you are considering. I would recommend weighing this against the other information you have collected about your role responsibilities and external applicability, career path, and relative compensation in making your final employment decision.

When I was trying to decide on a company with which to start my full-time career, I was very careful to consider each of the four factors discussed in this chapter. I was particularly focused on the responsibilities of the role relative to external corporations and career path opportunities that I could expect at the prospective employer beyond the initial role. During my interviews for full-time employment, I was careful to ask questions that provided the most information about and insight into these factors. I was then able to compare the information I gathered from several different prospective employers against the information I had gathered during my internship and subsequent full-time employment offer from this consumer products company. They were willing to provide me with significant details about the job opportunity relative to typical responsibilities, key customers, expected time in the position, an overall career ladder, and the potential for future advancement. I was also given the opportunity to speak with other individuals who had started in similar positions and see how their careers had progressed. From there, it was possible to somewhat crudely translate this information (along with information gathered in my internship) into expected work, learning opportunities, job applicability to future roles at this company as well as external environments, exposure to senior leadership, career flexibility, and overall fit. My conclusion was that this opportunity would provide me with a good foundation for future career growth and resulted in my accepting the offer for full-time employment. I am absolutely convinced that I would not have experienced the career progression that I have if I had not been as diligent in my initial employer assessment process.

Section 2
Early to Midcareer Management

This section of the book is designed to be used as a resource for individuals who are just entering or already into their career. However, for individuals still in school or looking to go back to school for a different or advanced degree to change careers, it contains very useful information as you near graduation. In some situations, this information might cause you to even rethink your approach to work and ultimately your decisions about school.

Chapter 9
How and Why to Impress Customers Early

Maximize Your First Impressions

In starting any new job or assignment, developing a favorable first impression often shapes the lens through which you are viewed for the foreseeable future. Frequently, the work you do early in your initial job at a particular company becomes the foundation for future opportunities. Therefore, it is crucial to make very positive first impressions. Ideally, these impressions will be memorable and create a positive "halo effect" that distinguishes you as a high-potential individual with unique talents—which will separate you from your peers as you strive to advance in your career goals.

Quickly impressing the "customers" of your work is one of the most effective methods for building trust and credibility in your capabilities. In a generic sense, "customers" include your current manager, as well as any other individuals who depend on the work you do for them. Getting "up-to-speed" as quickly as possible on your job requirements is generally the most critical first step in beginning a new role. This begins with determining how to complete your work efficiently and effectively with an appropriate level of accuracy or quality. While it is generally expected that a new employee will take some time to effectively transition into a new role, you really do not want to use this excuse for very long. In general and with any new role, it is wise to make a significant,

74

incremental investment of time to learn the role as quickly as possible in order to minimize any "start-up" curve and quickly impress customers with your capabilities.

In preparing for a new role—ideally even before you have started it—I recommend doing as much research and proactive self-education as possible to provide perspective, context, and background on the organization or group you will be joining and their objectives. Use available information—whether it is through contacts you already have in the new organization, or information you already have access to—in order to understand the strengths, weaknesses, and opportunities within this group. Where applicable, it will also be helpful to gain perspective on competition, benchmarks (internal and external), and industry best practices.

To be most effective when you start your new role and begin to understand the work requirements, I highly recommend that you consider the output of your work from your customers' perspectives. Understand what you are providing, and think about how it is currently being used. Similarly, consider the output of your work relative to what you would want if you were in the role of each of your customers. Additionally, assess the outputs of your work relative to what the *ideal* information would be in order to most effectively or optimally do that job. When you think about your work from this angle, you will generally find that there is a significant disconnect between what the customer is currently getting (or even content with), versus what the customer would ideally like to receive. It is common for customers to become content or perhaps "settle" for the information or work product that they are getting from the current incumbent. It is also relatively likely that your customers might not have thought through what would be the *ideal* information or work product to receive to best manage their jobs, particularly if this was the way your predecessor had managed it. However, identifying disconnects between what is *currently* being provided to customers and what could *ideally* be provided can often highlight opportunities that you may be able to effectively exploit. Developing solutions that will impress your customers early in your relationship and gain their trust and enhance your credibility are critical foundations for gaining sponsorship.

After assessing the work you are doing from a customer perspective, next consider the process that is used to create any job outputs. Start with the beginning of the process and document each step required in order to complete the outputs of your new job. (This may seem a bit menial at first, but this work can often highlight significant process "waste" that takes up time you could be spending on much more customer-valued work.) After you complete the process checklist, carefully assess the end output and how each step of the process contributes to the output. Consider whether there are opportunities to simplify and streamline the process by getting information from different sources or automating any elements of the process. Also, think about what information, work product or service does *not* create significant value for your customers (from their perspectives), but is relatively time-consuming to create, which provides an opportunity to simplify, streamline, or be eliminated. Simplification or optimization of inherited processes will generally gain support from your manager and often provide you with an opportunity to deliver outputs to customers on an accelerated timeline, which will not go unrecognized.

As you continue in the new job or role, do not lose your initial intensity or quest to uncover opportunities

76

to improve the job or provide better outputs to your customers. As you become more efficient at completing your routine responsibilities, use this time to proactively look for more opportunities and provide insights to your manager and customers. Make your manager and customers aware of your interest in taking on greater responsibilities, and find out what you can do to provide additional value for them. If they do not have any specific ideas, be creative and think about what you could do that they would value. Then, proactively develop them—most managers and customers will be ecstatic with this type of support.

Consistently Exceed Customer Expectations

Your ability to move into new and higher-level roles will be dependent upon not just your ability to impress customers quickly, but also your commitment to impressing them consistently. This will invariably mean demonstrating compelling work in a particular role or assignment for a reasonable period of time. *Complacency has no place in the vocabulary of an individual with aggressive career motivations.* You might not need to invest the same amount of time to do your job after awhile as you did when you first started it. However, you will want to ensure you are providing a similar level of customer service, maintaining a consistently positive attitude, and continuing to impress your manager and customers.

As an example, when I was transitioning from a more cost-focused role into a financial analyst role with complete responsibility for overall business performance, I was concerned about the significantly increased breadth of responsibility and knowledge required to do the new job. I knew that this had often been a difficult, yet critical, career transition for other employees. Thus, I wanted to do whatever I could to get "up-to-speed" on the job and start adding value quickly in order to ensure my transition was successful. Without any significant contacts in the business to provide perspective, I had to get creative. I knew that I had about a month before my transition would begin—so I wanted to take advantage of this and gain as much knowledge and insight into the new role as soon as possible.

As part of a large conglomerate corporation with common financial systems, I had access to detailed financial data for the new business that I would be supporting. I decided that the most effective way to learn the new business before taking on the new role would be to create an interactive financial model encompassing everything from sales by product format, customer pricing, manufacturing locations, and assets, all the way through product specifications. Developing this training material was quite time-consuming and required significant dedication outside of normal business hours, since I was still maintaining my previous job responsibilities. However, through this effort, I was able to develop a very solid foundation and background on the new business to make my transition virtually seamless.

As a result of my prework, I was able to quickly provide new and unexpected insights to my customers. Rather than trying to learn a "foreign" business while receiving training on my new job responsibilities, I almost immediately began working to understand customer needs and assess gaps in what they were receiving and what they really wanted or needed. As a result of this prework, I was able to quickly improve the level of service provided to customers, gaining sponsorship and leadership in the business, which ultimately resulted in my being quickly promoted into another opportunity ahead of my peers and my own aggressive expectations.

Chapter 10
Building and Exploiting Exposure to Gain Sponsorship

Impressing your customers is absolutely critical to ensure success in your current role. However, even extremely positive customer feedback might not be enough to be considered for new and better opportunities if you and your work have not been exposed to the appropriate decision makers.

Sometimes exposure to individuals who will either determine or heavily influence future promotional opportunities comes naturally with a job. However, ideal exposure opportunities are less common and more infrequent than you might like. Therefore, you must be prepared to exploit these opportunities when they do come up.

One of the first things to recognize about exposure is that the quality of the work that you produce and the impressions that you make are what counts. As discussed in chapter 9: "How and Why to Impress Customers Early," good early impressions often create a positive halo effect that in some ways is difficult to change. The opposite is also *very* true. Therefore, you should make every effort to provide the most favorable impression at every exposure opportunity—even if you are just starting a new job or role and the expectations are not high. In fact, creating an extremely favorable early impression is a way to really highlight your unique capabilities—particularly if you can back this up with consistently favorable impressions at future exposure times.

Ultimately, you want to exploit exposure opportunities with those individuals who can most directly and effectively influence your career, and who you believe could become strong sponsors. To increase your effectiveness at maximizing exposure opportunities and gaining sponsorship from influential leaders, I recommend taking an active, three-step approach. First, determine which leaders you will need to gain exposure to and sponsorship from in order to be considered for better, future career opportunities. Second, develop a strategy for best taking advantage of exposure opportunities that are presented to you with the leaders you identified from step one. Third, determine how you may proactively "create" exposure opportunities with those individuals whom you identified in step one. By actively identifying those individuals who might most directly influence your career and developing a plan to impress them with your unique skills, you should greatly increase your likelihood of gaining better career opportunities at an accelerated pace.

Step 1: Identify Potential Sponsors

The ideal situation is to impress all of the people with whom you interact in your job on a daily basis with consistently extraordinary work. However, the reality for most individuals with limited time is that you need to be somewhat selective about where you choose to invest your time. Given this constraint, you must clearly understand where to *best* make incremental investments to ensure your work is effectively showcased to those individuals who are most important to influencing your career. This starts with understanding which individuals are most critical to receive support from in order to gain sponsorship.

Generally, creating a lasting, positive impression on anyone at a higher level than you in an organization is ideal. However, this is often not realistic and also not required. It is far better and more pragmatic to understand which individuals are most likely to have a *direct* influence on your career. Creating consistently positive, lasting impressions with these individuals should be a primary focus.

As basic as this sounds, identifying targeted sponsors should begin with understanding the organizational chart within your particular functional area (e.g., marketing, sales, finance, supply chain, etc.), as well as within any other functional areas that you closely work with in your current role.

It is almost a given that the first person on your list of targeted sponsors will be your current manager. However, beyond your current manager, you will want to gain a clear sense for the key decision makers and influencers of future opportunities and roles. Depending on the organization, it is likely that promotional opportunities are not simply a function of your current manager's desires, but will require the endorsement of other functional leaders several levels above your particular manager.

While your manager might have the influence to independently persuade these other leaders, your likelihood of success will be significantly increased if your work and capabilities have been favorably viewed by this leadership group. Thus, you should gain an understanding of the organizational design within your functional area and the styles and general expectations of these individuals, including the level of influence of every individual and their historical willingness to provide sponsorship for people they have strong opinions about. To the extent that you currently have or can gain exposure to some of these decision makers, you should consider these factors.

Ultimately, your capabilities and work product might be perceived as more valuable to some leaders than others. I recommend finding ways to showcase your work, skills, and capabilities to those individuals who have capabilities that most closely align with your own. Ideally, these leaders will be some of the more influential within the group of decision makers that you identified previously as potential targeted sponsors. If not, you will have to further develop capabilities and competencies in order to gain credibility with these influential decision makers.

One additional consideration worth mentioning is the level of influence and credibility of your current manager. Understanding your direct manager's level of respect and credibility as it relates to talent identification is particularly important if you have limited exposure to other critical, potential sponsors. Trying to ascertain this can be a bit difficult and will generally need to be inferred based on promotions and the placement of other talented individuals who also previously reported to your manager. If you believe that you will need considerable sponsorship beyond your manager due to his or her lack of support, then it will be absolutely critical that you maximize those exposure opportunities that you do get with other potential sponsors. Further, "creating" additional exposure opportunities will be that much more important (to be discussed later in this chapter).

Step 2: Maximize Exposure Opportunities

Opportunities to gain exposure to prominent and influential leaders can come at different times, sometimes when it is somewhat unexpected or even inopportune. However, when exposure opportunities become available, it is imperative that you make the most of them. Often these situations are available more frequently than people realize, but in a form that on the surface may not appear like opportunities.

In reality, virtually any exposure to an individual who can influence your future career opportunities (likely identified as a potential sponsor previously in step 1) should be considered an opportunity. Some exposure opportunities are fairly straightforward, such as a one-on-one meeting with a potential sponsor. However, other good exposure opportunities include lunches, dinners, presentations, business trips, volunteering activities, or any other event that provides an opportunity to interact with individuals who are likely to have influence on your career.

The key is to be prepared as much as possible when these exposure opportunities arise in order to ensure you *garner support* from your potential sponsors—not just face time. Whatever the opportunity, seriously preparing in advance for identified exposure opportunities is in your best interest—recalling that these opportunities are any situation that involves interaction with a potential sponsor or leader who can influence your career.

Frequently, people dismiss very good exposure opportunities because they do not appropriately recognize them. As an example, several years ago, I was invited along with a few other individuals to a lunch with the chief financial officer in the organization where I was working. Most of the individuals going to this lunch had not previously received much exposure to this leader, including me. With about a week's advance notice of this event, it occurred to me that this lunch was really a *disguised opportunity* for me to showcase some of my work and skills. This was clearly *not* about having a free lunch or just an opportunity to meet the CFO.

To prepare for the lunch, I made a list of the work that I was currently doing in my organization that I thought the senior leader might be interested in, with a focus on activities that were unique, creative, self-initiated, and already implemented successfully or in the process of being implemented. I summarized the top four examples and arranged them on an index card that I could discretely bring with me to the lunch and place on my lap. At the lunch, while many of the other individuals dominated their discussion time with topics such as college sports or general inquiries about the senior leader's perspective on current events, I kept my focus clearly on my agenda, being careful to find ways to seamlessly weave it into the conversation. In reality, interjecting work and business topics was fairly easy—as this was exactly where the CFO wanted the conversation to go—if it weren't evident by his body language, it was clear that he continued to push the conversation in this direction when he had the opportunity.

By preparing in advance for this lunch and staying focused on the true objective, I was able to turn a free lunch into a very positive exposure opportunity that (along with several other positive interactions) ultimately helped lead to sponsorship from the CFO, whose support was critical to many of my subsequent career moves.

The key takeaway from this example is that if you have the opportunity to interact with an influential, potential sponsor, creatively think through how you can capitalize on the situation—even if it doesn't seem ideal by traditional standards.

Step 3: Create Exposure Opportunities

Sometimes exposure opportunities come less frequently than you desire—even when you are thinking creatively about taking advantage of volunteering activities, meals, or other nontraditional events. This can be especially true when your targeted sponsors (from step 1) do not work in close proximity to your business or team—or are less engaged with you or your team for whatever reason. In this situation, "creating" exposure can be one of the most effective methods for gaining access to a targeted potential sponsor.

Begin by assessing what you believe would garner favorable interest from your targeted sponsor(s). First work to ascertain the interests of this particular leader or leaders. Most individuals who have risen to the ranks as leaders are going to be interested in activities, research, insights, etc., that will deliver results to enable them to continue to ascend in an organization, or at a minimum, maintain their current position. Therefore, understanding some of the issues and problems that they are trying to solve or that they see as opportunities from their vantage points should be a focus for you. Anything that you believe you could do to improve business performance (particularly if it is an immediate benefit with minimal investment) should receive attention from these leaders. However, if these leaders have accountabilities for special projects, networks, or other activities (which most do), these could provide other avenues for positive exposure.

Of particular focus should be those areas where you: 1) have an inherent strength (and ideally, interest) that you can effectively showcase; 2) where this strength or interest can tie in (at least loosely) with an opportunity or issue that you currently have been tasked with developing, leading, or solving as part of your normal job responsibilities; and 3) where you have the time and resources to sufficiently create something that is truly unique and compelling enough to garner the attention and favor of the targeted sponsor(s). It is not necessarily bad if the exposure that you can create comes through a network or special project—you just might have to do a bit of work to ensure that the exposure that you gain in this capacity will translate into sponsorship in your job.

The next challenge is to determine how to get this work in front of your targeted sponsor(s). This step can sometimes require a bit of creativity—particularly if the access to your targeted sponsor(s) is very limited. However, if you have effectively developed a truly compelling solution to an opportunity or problem where you believe the sponsor(s) has(ve) a significant interest (validated by appropriate due diligence), this is a very good foundation. To be clear, your work should not just be good. If you want to be fairly certain that you will gain the attention of your targeted sponsor(s), you must ensure that the work you showcase is truly unique and exceptional—and it must be perceived as such. This means that the content must be clearly articulated and in a way that will be intuitive to leadership—and in a manner that is memorable and will "draw in" your audience. This will be critical to getting your manager or other customers

87

to want to share this with other leaders (including your targeted sponsor or sponsors).

If your work is something that is highly unique, compelling, and intuitive for them to easily share with more senior leaders, then it will generally help them to look good and increase the likelihood that they will share it. (To make sure you are being perfectly honest with yourself, one question to ask yourself before presenting your work is, "How truly unique is my project versus others that my manager and customers are used to seeing?" Until you can honestly answer yourself that this is truly a standout piece of work, then you probably have a bit more enhancing to do.)

Don't concern yourself with whether the work you did may also make your immediate manager or customers look good or highlight their involvement, which might not have been much. The key concern is that you get your work shared with your targeted sponsor(s). The best-case scenario is that you gain the opportunity to directly present your work to these targeted sponsor(s). Don't be passive about this. Instead, as you initially present your work to your customers or manager, highlight the interest that you believe your targeted sponsor(s) might also have in it, and clearly indicate your interest in presenting your work to them yourself. If your customers or manager see the value of the work and opportunity, as well as your interest in getting exposure to your targeted sponsor(s) early on, this will clearly increase your probability of gaining the opportunity to present this work to more senior leaders.

If this approach to gaining exposure to the sponsor(s) does not ultimately play out as you desire, and you strongly believe that there would be considerable interest in your work if seen by your targeted sponsor(s), there still are other avenues to achieve your objective. This is where understanding what networks or other projects your target(s) may be involved in can be useful— in particular, if you have access to them. While not as direct of an approach, many organizations and some project teams will welcome involvement of new volunteers. (You don't have to necessarily share a significant passion on the topics, though it would be ideal if you did.) Volunteering to join a network, organization, or project with the target sponsor(s) may create the opportunity for an introduction. This should provide a very good avenue to speak with your sponsor target(s) directly and provide a brief (and well-rehearsed but casual) "elevator speech" about some of the work that you are doing. Volunteering to set up some time with them to take them through the work in a less informal setting will likely be positively received if there is some genuine interest by the targeted sponsor.

Finally, once you get the opportunity to present your work, recommendation, opportunities, etc., to your targeted sponsor(s), make sure to truly capitalize on this exposure opportunity. Regardless of any other job responsibilities that you have at the time, maximizing this exposure opportunity will almost certainly be more important and impactful from a career standpoint. If you want to turn this exposure opportunity into sponsorship (which will be crucial to moving your career along at an accelerated rate), then you must capitalize on your time with this potential sponsor. My advice would be to prepare for this type of interaction like it were a final exam. This is not something that you want to take lightly—as the positive "halo" that you are attempting to create can also have an equally significant opposite effect if you do not deliver. Consider your content, your method of delivery, the interest of your audience, likely questions, and what you can do to make this experience memorable and highly compelling. This interaction was the ultimate goal of all your previous hard work, so you will want to make sure that you take it across the finish line and achieve your objective of turning a targeted *potential* sponsor into an *actual* sponsor.

As an example of how I used these techniques to gain exposure and sponsorship, early in my career, I was looking for an opportunity to better showcase my capabilities and skills to company leaders. My direct manager had recognized my work as being strong, but I did not have a tremendous amount of exposure to the more senior leadership that would be required for getting promoted to a higher level. I had been proactively working on a business simulation and analytics tool that I believed had the potential to be very powerful for both strategic and tactical management in the facility where I worked, as well as for others at higher levels within the business, including some of the more senior leaders that I hoped to gain exposure to and ultimately career sponsorship from. While my current manager was clearly in support of this work, he was looking for something that was fairly simple and that could be used to help answer some fairly basic questions.

Early into the development of this simulation project, I recognized that the time investment required to complete this tool was going to be significant, and that I would not likely find the time to complete it during normal work hours. However, in assessing the senior leadership in my functional area, this project seemed like a really good fit—as one of the individuals had previously been instrumental in the development of some significant financial systems that provided a more systematic way to analyze product supply costs. Another leader, whom I saw as a bit of a visionary within the company (and who himself had considerable sponsorship and was willing to aggressively sponsor others), was generally looking for creative, new ways to more effectively deliver performance improvements. This simulation tool seemed like something that would align well with both of these individuals and something that I expected they would have interest in seeing if I were to create it. Therefore, I decided that the time investment on evenings, weekends, and even vacation days would be worth it if it led to the exposure, and ultimately sponsorship, that I believed I could achieve with it.

Upon completing the project and sharing it with my facility team, interest from individuals in other parts of the organization grew, including some of the functional leaders that I had hoped to gain exposure to through this project. This gave me the opportunity to present my work directly to several influential leaders and highlight my systems, analytical, and presentation skills. The reaction from these leaders was quite favorable, and I was offered a double promotion to a new role with greater responsibilities shortly thereafter.

This example illustrates the merit of each step discussed earlier in the chapter, starting with the development of an understanding of the leadership and key decision makers who can influence new job opportunities. It also highlights the value of selecting sponsor "targets" to whom you ideally want to showcase your skills and work. Finally, it speaks to the importance of maximizing exposure when available, and proactively creating opportunities for exposure to those leaders, and ultimately decision makers, who are not otherwise accessible. While this approach requires incremental time investments at strategic points, I have found it to be extremely effective for me and others who want to gain greater exposure and ultimately develop the sponsorship that is generally required to advance quickly in an organization.

Chapter 11
Managing Perceptions

While clearly not true in all situations, perceptions can become reality when it comes to performance, achievement, and personal "branding" in a work environment. This is particularly true in large, complex organizations. Therefore, understanding and "managing" how you are perceived by others can ensure you maintain the career trajectory that you desire.

Step 1: Understand How You Are Perceived

Understanding others' perceptions of you is the first step in managing perceptions. Of particular interest is to gain an understanding of the perceptions of influential senior leaders, such as the targeted sponsor(s) who were discussed in chapter 10: "Building and Exploiting Exposure to Gain Sponsorship." Outside of directly asking for candid feedback about what you can do better (which I would encourage you to frequently do), understanding perceptions sometimes will require you to interpret more subtle clues.

Whenever possible, it is advisable to ask for feedback from peers, customers, supervisors, and anyone else whose opinions you value. This should not be limited to just those individuals who will provide you with feedback you want to hear. The most important feedback (and that which is sometimes most impactful to perceptions) can come from individuals whom you don't always agree with, or who can give you candid, constructive feedback. Not all feedback is created equally, and you will need to almost certainly do some filtering. However, building a periodic mechanism for gathering feedback is a great method for ensuring that you have a sense for how you are being perceived (and also what you are doing well and what you could improve).

Gathering feedback from more senior leaders with whom you do not have much exposure, with whom you do not have a relationship, or from whom you don't feel comfortable directly asking for feedback, may be a bit more challenging. However, there are other methods for gathering feedback that are often not considered as such. There are two mechanisms that typically provide very good avenues for assessing your perception by leaders. The first involves the typically annual employee performance review process. (This is often very challenging for many individuals when they are being evaluated but it can truly be highly valuable if viewed as an opportunity rather than a critique.) Keep a very open mind to consider the feedback that you are presented from the standpoint of potential sponsorship and how you are being perceived. Is the feedback and rating consistent with what you honestly expected? What is the feedback on different elements of your performance, particularly those that involved exposure to influential leaders? Try to consider these and other questions as you review feedback and determine what elements you may want to focus on improving.

The second area of potentially valuable, indirect feedback on sponsorship and your perceptions comes with longer-range discussions about career moves. Consider what opportunities are being brought to you as likely next roles, and how this compares to your expectations in terms of the quality of opportunities, as well as their timing. If you believe that there are different or better opportunities for which you should be considered, try to find out why you were not considered. As you go through this process, you must keep an open mind and assess the feedback objectively. I would encourage you to keep notes of your conversations that include likely next roles; what would need to occur for these new roles to come to fruition (including what you would need to deliver or do); and likely timing. As these and other roles become available, assess how your career discussion has played out in terms of timing, and whether you were considered for these opportunities, or if the jobs went to other candidates.

Your goal here is not to debate the feedback or processes, but rather to get clarity on how you are perceived (not just by what you are told, but also by what you see happening in terms of new opportunities becoming available to you, and their timing). The key to all of this feedback is to look for "hidden" themes that provide perspective on how you are perceived both today and as it relates to future opportunities. This will help you ultimately determine how to best use this information in your career management process.

Step 2: Managing Others' Perceptions of You

After you have a baseline and process for assessing where you stand and what others' perceptions of you are, the next step is to ensure you have a process for managing your behaviors and actions to create the beliefs that you want, while still being true to yourself.

First, from the direct and indirect feedback you gathered, assess whether the perceptions of you are accurate. This personal assessment will only be useful if you are honest with yourself, as it will be the baseline for what actions you take next. If you feel the assessment is accurate, it is worthwhile contemplating *why* you believe the perceptions are accurate. In other words, is there something that you have done to ensure that you are viewed as you would expect? If the viewpoints are accurate and positive, is there something that you are doing that you should ensure that you continue doing? While it can be very easy to assume there is no follow-up needed if you are being positively perceived, understanding *why* is valuable. Without an understanding of why you are being perceived favorably, it will be difficult to know conclusively what you have been doing that has resulted in favorable impressions and further ensure that you can maintain these perceptions going forward.

Alternatively, if the perceptions of you and your work are unfavorable, then the next question to consider is whether they are consistent with reality. In either case, it is important to get an understanding of the gap, as well as perspective, on whether this is something that you believe you can realistically change.

If you truly do not believe that you can change either the performance or perception (for whatever reason), then it is probably time to think through whether you are in the right role to showcase your capabilities and gain the sponsorship needed to advance to the next level. (This is also discussed in chapter 15: "Why and When to Change Jobs.")

If your manager, customers, or more importantly, targeted sponsors, appear to have a negative perception of you that you believe are incorrect and that you can change, then you must build a plan to shift this perception to a positive one that is more consistent with reality (assuming you believe you can change their beliefs). My experience suggests that limited exposure based on minor interactions with you and your work and performance are frequently extrapolated into beliefs and can be one of the biggest reasons for perception gaps. This is also one of the easiest areas to correct, as it starts with actively pursuing additional exposure. Of course, it will be imperative that you carefully consider how to best capitalize on this exposure to ensure interactions are highly positive, especially since you are trying to change an existing belief. (Chapter 10: "Building and Exploiting Exposure to Gain Sponsorship," is a good reference for how to effectively increase exposure opportunities and capitalize on them.) Even in situations where perception gaps exist because of limited exposure, you still must understand what interactions or behaviors might have resulted in the forming of negative perceptions; this is something that you definitely want to be mindful of when you have new exposure opportunities.

If negative perceptions are not simply a function of extrapolations based on limited exposure, then there is generally more work that needs to be done to improve the situation. In this case, it is worthwhile to again ask yourself why a negative perception exists that is inconsistent with reality and confirm that this is just a perception and not reality. With that said, the solution is essentially the same in either case: you will want to understand the root cause and build a plan to address it with those individuals who have a negative perception (particularly anyone who will have an influence on your future career progression).

Changing *deep-rooted* perceptions can be very challenging and take considerable time. Numerous favorable interactions are usually needed to change such attitudes and beliefs. This does not mean that it is not possible; I can speak to this from my own personal experience where I worked close to two years to change the perceptions of some influential senior leaders about my potential and capabilities. In my situation, I had created a belief that I was very strong on systems, tools, and analytics but there was a question about whether I could be a good manager of others. I knew that I could be a good manager and so it was simply a question of how to best gain the opportunity to showcase this. However, I also recognized that demonstrating this capability would require me to over-deliver versus what is traditionally expected (i.e., I would need to show not just that I was competent as a manager but that I was exceptionally strong at leading a team, building talent, and getting results through others).

To accomplish this, I needed to first have a team to manage—something that I knew might be difficult if there was a question about whether I was better suited to be an individual contributor. (This was further complicated by the limited number of manager positions within the relatively flat organizational structure in the group where I worked.) Therefore, I needed to be a bit pragmatic about how to show that I could be a good manager. I started small by asking to lead a project that was suited to my skills but required support from two to three other analysts. I proposed that I lead this project but asked my manager for the other analysts to *indirectly* work for me, taking work direction from me throughout the duration of the project. This was a fairly low risk scenario for my manager and provided a good test for me in a managerial capacity. Clearly we needed to deliver on the project. However, I needed to step back and avoid the temptation to default to solving all of the challenges myself. Instead, I forced myself to operate at a higher level and work with the team to help solve the different problems relative to concept development, design, and execution. Throughout this project I devoted a significant amount of time to working with the individual team members to build their capabilities and help them with different elements of the project where they needed additional support. Ultimately, we effectively completed the project and received several accolades for the work. More significant, however, was that I was able to showcase my skills as a manager and change the beliefs of the leaders in my function about the breadth of my capabilities. Shortly thereafter, I was given a team of analysts to manage and have managed progressively larger teams ever since.

Be prepared for what it will take to change beliefs and perceptions—at times it might be incredibly frustrating. To change perceptions, it is critical to maintain composure and focus on this objective and on the changes that you determine are required (based on your assessment of the gap in reality). Nonetheless, if your efforts are successful, it is highly likely that you will create a lasting, positive "halo effect" that will gain you sponsorship from many of the same individuals who initially would have been potential roadblocks to your career advancement.

Chapter 12
Building Your Resume While at Work

One of the best pieces of advice that I received from one of my professors upon graduating was to "make sure that whatever job you take throughout your career, you continue to learn." I have tried to keep this in mind during my career. However, after going through an external job search following my time at the software start-up, it became clear to me that this advice required a bit of augmenting. In addition to ensuring that new job opportunities will help to advance your learning, it is also very critical to think about how the role will impact your resume from both an internal and external company standpoint. Rather than building your resume *after* you have completed an assignment or project, you should think about what work will help you to make your resume (as well as your skills) stronger and select roles or projects that will enable this.

Assessing Opportunities

Before taking a new job or project with your existing employer or a new employer, assess what you believe the role affords you in terms of two or three "bullets" to add to your resume, and how prospective future employers would view them. (This applies whether or not you have any intentions to stay with your current employer long-term.) Considerations should include: the organization as well as its reputation; the size and scope of the new role; recent performance trends and expected future performance; job responsibilities; and whether you are managing a team (and the size and skill set of that group).

You will want to think about what types of unique opportunities the role presents (i.e., understand what you can make of the role beyond its position description). This can depend on the normal responsibilities of the role, as well as the flexibility of your prospective manager and customers. Understanding and weighing each of these factors will help you assess whether a role will provide you with the ability to truly build your resume to the extent that you desire.

Keeping an external perspective in mind is always important to ensure future career flexibility. When evaluating potential roles or projects, consider the value that the opportunities afforded in this work would have to employers outside of your current organization (i.e., How would the "bullets" on your resume look to a hiring manager at another company? Would the sequence of experiences show career ascension or would they create questions about success and sponsorship?). This is a very good test to apply as you consider new opportunities.

In chapter 8: "Selecting a Job", guidance was provided on helping you to select an employer based on a number of factors including company recognition, career progression opportunities, and the type of work and experiences you would likely gain. In a similar fashion, you will want to consider how different roles or opportunities will impact your resume. Putting yourself in the shoes of a prospective hiring manager, assess how new opportunities would likely be viewed. A few questions to consider include the following:

- *Are the roles and responsibilities of the individual clearly increasing over time, suggesting a personal commitment to growth and organizational sponsorship?*
- *Do position and/or organization changes and transitions appear logical?*
- *Do role transitions suggest the individual has clear career purpose and drive or do moves seem more random in nature?*

As much as possible, it is useful to assess potential opportunities from the perspective of an outside company that might be considering candidates for an open position. With this in mind, even roles that may be considered highly valuable to your current employer from a developmental or even promotional perspective may not be logical to an external company. In this situation, it may be a bit more difficult to decide how to best proceed but it is still useful to understand the differences.

As an example, in one business unit where I worked there was a high value placed on taking international assignments to broaden career perspectives as the sector was working to expand more of its operations globally. However, many of the opportunities were dramatically smaller in scope, business size, team size, etc. versus those within the United States. Nonetheless, this was becoming increasingly important for advancement within this business unit. While this international work experience would likely be considered a positive attribute to have at many other companies, it did not have the same importance—and from a resume standpoint, taking on such an opportunity (with significantly smaller role dimensions) may have raised questions about sponsorship, career opportunities, and

102

ultimately my value. As a result, I chose to pass on several opportunities that were presented to me and instead focused on roles that I believed would be valued highly not just internally but also externally.

Allocating Your Time to Resume Building Activities

One of the biggest mistakes that I typically see individuals make is to assume that their resumes are simply going to build themselves based on the roles they have taken. While selecting the right roles is definitely the first step in building your resume, you will need to make sure that you have something to talk about that is truly unique and compelling (this applies to both opportunities at your current employer, as well as externally).

As you consider your personal objectives and the projects on which you work, think about how these would be viewed on your resume. This should provide some perspective about where you are focusing your time and energy. However, don't just stop there. The biggest opportunities (and frequently the ones that are missed) are often uncovered by asking the question, "What major accomplishments would I ideally like to be able to attach to this job on my resume?" Instead of doing your job and updating your resume after it is complete, this approach starts with the end in mind. Consider what two or three items you would hope to be able to include on your resume after a successful year in the assignment. (It is clearly useful if these personal priorities are aligned with those of your internal customers and manager—and if you can gain alignment on these objectives—even if it means putting in considerable incremental time to accomplish them.) While it is likely that unforeseen priorities may

103

cause you to deviate somewhat from your plan, this will provide a roadmap for you and help you to stay focused on your objectives. The biggest challenge will be how to allocate as much of your time as possible to these resume-building activities. This is something that may take a daily commitment to ensure that you consider what you are working on and how you are prioritizing to put the maximum amount of time towards those activities that will be highly valued on your resume.

In addition to building a stronger resume, it is likely that this approach will also ensure that you are spending your time on activities that are more valuable to your internal customers as well as in your development and recognition.

Chapter 13
Core Competencies and Competitive Advantages

It is interesting to me how many individuals don't truly know what their core competencies (or strengths) are relative to their peers or their impact on organizational performance. What is perhaps more surprising is that those individuals who *do* understand their strengths often spend a disproportionate amount of time looking for roles and opportunities to "broaden" their skill sets, with much of the focus on where they are perhaps only mildly deficient and often where they do not enjoy working.

Having a strong understanding of your core competencies and competitive advantages versus peers and other leaders is absolutely critical to ensuring you take on roles, projects, and even a career path that will provide you with the level of advancement desired. Whether or not you realize it, *you* are likely in the best position to do a true assessment of your strengths. This could range from specific technical skills to leadership attributes or communication capabilities. In doing a skills assessment, consider how you compare against peers and more senior leaders (all the way up through your most aspirational career role). After you have completed this independent assessment of your core competencies and competitive advantages, there is generally some value to asking others to assess you, too, especially your direct manager, peers, or others who have interacted with you considerably, ideally over the course of several roles. This assessment from others will be a good test to: 1) validate your own assumptions and see if there are any other major competencies or competitive advantages that others see but that you simply did not consider; and 2) determine whether there is a gap between your beliefs and the perceptions of others. (If a significant perception gap exists, chapter 11: "Managing Perceptions," may be a good resource to reference in terms of how to mitigate this situation.)

As you gain clarity on your true core competencies (particularly those where you have a significant advantage over your peers or more senior leaders), you must determine how you will best showcase them within the context of your work. Further, your primary focus should be building a plan to best use these skills and attributes to help you advance through the different roles you need to attain your desired career objectives (which includes everything from interviewing to selecting projects to focus areas in future roles). It may be helpful to reference the targeted career progression map that you developed in chapter 2: "Goal Setting and Management," and for each major milestone role, consider what attributes are critical to your success. To the extent you can, thinking through how you can use your true core competencies and competitive advantages (and building a plan to leverage them) will almost certainly guarantee that you deliver the desired results and are perceived in the most positive manner.

While I would not advocate completely ignoring your weaknesses, understanding which ones will be exposed throughout your targeted career path evolution will help to prioritize where to focus, so you do not invest incremental time in areas that are not critical to your success. Instead, this time can be used for additional work and activities (ideally taking advantage of your core competencies) that will create greater sponsorship and future career advancement opportunities.

There are countless examples of where I have seen very talented individuals with fairly specialized skillsets (e.g., tax, controllership, B2B marketing, etc.) take on a series of lateral moves to gain greater, broader experiences in different areas in the hope that this would help them to advance more rapidly. Unfortunately, I can only think of a very limited number of these individuals that were able to excel in different disciplines, thus propelling their careers. (In these situations, the successful individuals generally had a skillset that was not unique to a particular function but rather was transferable across many. One individual was an incredibly effective problem-solver, while another had a unique skill for inspiring teams through highly compelling communication.) However, most of the examples with whom I have worked would have been better served to recognize their unique skills and invest time to become the best they could in their areas of interest and specialty. One caveat to this would be when the career path in an area of specialty may be limited in an organization. In this situation, a more diverse career path may be the only realistic opportunity for advancement—or may require you to change companies to one where there is more advancement potential.

The key is to ensure that you understand your unique competencies and how they can be potentially exploited to help you rapidly advance along your targeted career path—and that you carefully contemplate this as you build your career map and plans for achieving desired levels of progression.

Chapter 14
When to Consider an MBA

Considering whether to get an MBA is a question many individuals ponder at some point, usually after they conclude an undergraduate degree or after starting a career. Gaining exposure to the fundamentals of business and management often provides an extremely valuable perspective. This advanced education can be useful for individuals looking to change careers, as well as for those who want to gain a greater perspective on broad or specific business management concepts that provide potential for further career advancement. Pursuing an MBA will generally require a significant time and financial investment. Therefore, it is worthwhile to have a clear plan for what you would like to get out of the program in advance, validate the reasonableness of your expectations, understand the opportunity costs, and develop a plan for how to best exploit your investment if you ultimately do pursue an MBA. The remainder of this chapter will focus on a logical process for assessing the pros and cons of pursuing an MBA (or any other investment in an advanced educational degree, for that matter). The goal will be to use data to take the emotion out of the process and allow you to make the optimal decision for your particular situation.

What to Expect from an MBA Program

Before deciding to enter an MBA program, it is important that you have a clear understanding of what you are hoping to accomplish by earning an MBA. Having this perspective will ensure you are making the right investments and that you are targeting your efforts against the appropriate specialization for you, focusing on the most appropriate activities to guarantee you achieve your objectives.

Consistent with the guidance on career goal setting and management (from chapter 2), I recommend starting with the end in mind when thinking through what you want to achieve with an MBA. In other words, consider what you are hoping the MBA will enable you to do that you cannot with your current education. Before even thinking about an MBA, you should have a clear understanding of where you want to go with your career. At a minimum, you need to know where you want to specialize with your MBA to get maximum value when you apply it in the workplace. Referencing the milestones and goals you identified as part of chapter 2: "Goal Setting and Management," should help to provide some of this context on where to focus and ideally *when* an MBA will provide the greatest benefit within your career progression. It may also help provide some perspective on what program will deliver the greatest benefit toward achieving your career objectives.

Throughout this assessment process, it is beneficial to evaluate the validity and reasonableness of your expectations in terms of what you expect the MBA will provide relative to your goals, particularly as it relates to advancement opportunities, compensation, and career flexibility. If you ultimately choose to enter an MBA program, I cannot over emphasize the value of maintaining a steady focus on how to best attain these goals throughout the entire program.

Opportunity Cost Considerations

Like any decision, there are "investment" costs that should be carefully considered before pursuing an MBA program. There are the financial outlay costs, which are generally pretty clear and which most individuals carefully consider before embarking on an MBA. Then there are the costs of time or money that otherwise could be invested in alternative activities, or the "opportunity costs." In my experience, few individuals truly consider the full opportunity costs of a decision to invest in an MBA program. Given the significant time and financial requirements required to earn an MBA, this decision is definitely one that should be contemplated in a logical, holistic manner.

Before deciding to embark on an MBA program, make sure to estimate the time required to complete the work. Consider not just the classroom time, but also studies (homework, reading, projects, etc.), examinations, and even travel or commuting time. Don't forget to include the investment of time in studying for the GMAT exam (which is required for most MBA programs as part of the application process); entrance applications; campus visits; and interviews. When you add up all the time, I would expect the hours to total between twenty-five hundred and five thousand, depending on the particular program that you are considering and whether it is full- or part-time (with more than one thousand hours being added to *normal* working hours, even with a part-time program). However, you should do your own estimate based on the information relevant to the particular program that you are considering—as requirements can differ significantly by school and program.

In the same manner as you estimated the time investment, consider the financial investment. Attempt to estimate not just the tuition, books, and other specific costs of the MBA program (though these should be included), but also think about any other costs that you might incur as a result of the MBA that you would not incur if you took a different career path (e.g., relocation costs, travel, etc.). Finally, consider the compensation you are losing by enrolling in the MBA program (this might only apply if you are considering a full-time program or if your hours and compensation are reduced because of the requirements of a part-time MBA program).

After assembling a holistic picture of the *full* costs of an MBA investment (both the direct financial outlay and opportunity costs), you will be in a better position to objectively and fully evaluate the potential investment in time and money. The key question to consider is: What *could* you alternatively do with the likely thousands of incremental hours of time and tens of thousands of dollars that you are considering investing in an MBA program?

For individuals who are already on a desirable career path with clear visibility into future growth opportunities that align with their targeted career goals, the question of opportunity costs should be very carefully considered. In this situation, an important question to contemplate is: If you were to make the same incremental *time* investments in your current job (e.g., taking on more responsibilities, leading additional projects, etc.) that you are considering for the MBA, what would the likely outcome be? Separately, if you were to make the same *financial* investments that you were considering for your MBA in focused training, education, or coaching relative to your specific opportunity areas (e.g., leadership, strategy, management, etc.), how would the outcome likely differ?

These are questions that many individuals do not frequently consider before making the decision to begin an MBA program. However, these questions should definitely be asked and contemplated carefully before making an investment, especially if you are already on an accelerated career path at your current employer and you believe that the time investment in an MBA might take away from your ability to do your job as effectively as you would like. In this case, pursuing an MBA might still make good sense at some point, but carefully consider *when* it makes the most sense, being cautious not to disrupt an already accelerated career path—particularly if a fast-track career progression is a major reason for wanting to invest in an MBA.

The ultimate test to validate your thinking on whether to invest the time and money on an MBA versus continuing with your current career path may be objectively conducting a full financial analysis. A full financial assessment is calculated by taking the financial outlay and opportunity costs of the MBA program relative to your current job or other potentially attractive alternatives. Offset this with any potential, incremental income you expect as a result of completing the MBA (whether at your current employer or a different employer). In each scenario, don't forget to consider the level of risk associated with each assumption and the relative value of each one on the overall conclusion.

To simplify the process of doing an MBA financial investment analysis, I have broken the process down into seven steps and have constructed a simple example. In

112

this example, I have assumed that the individual is currently employed and has an annual salary (before taxes) of $75,000 with an effective income tax rate of 33 percent (federal at nearly 20 percent, state at just over 7 percent, and social security around 6 percent). I have also assumed that this individual can expect annual promotions and associated raises of 5 percent in each future year with this current employer, suggesting aggressive career aspirations and potential. This individual is considering a part-time MBA program that could be completed in one year during weekends and evenings with minimal expected loss of income. A second scenario being considered is a two-year, full-time MBA program, which requires the individual to be 100 percent dedicated to school (i.e., there are no supplemental income opportunities). (It should be noted that this example is purely for illustrative purposes. Please consider your own unique situation and assumptions and develop your own MBA "valuation," as this will greatly impact the outcome of the exercise, with different decisions and situations having very different potential valuations.)

Step 1: Establish a Baseline, After-Tax Income

Establishing a baseline income will require you to determine what you would be doing if you were not pursuing an MBA. If you are currently employed, this would likely mean maintaining employment in your current job. In this situation, simply calculate your expected annual income associated with this job. If you are graduating from school, this may entail developing an educated guess as to the type of employment you could achieve with your level of education and the associated

113

annual income that you could reasonably anticipate. In either situation, understanding your baseline income will be very important for doing an appropriate financial analysis—this will provide the reference you will compare the value of your various MBA scenarios against. In the example that I described earlier, the individual's baseline income is derived from the current job—as if an MBA were not being pursued. Therefore, income is $75,000 before taxes or $50,250 after applying an estimated 33 percent effective income tax rate. Calculating income on an after-tax basis is important to make sure that all opportunities are compared on an equal basis, particularly if different levels of compensation put you into different tax brackets. (Please note that all examples included in this book are for illustrative purposes only. It is highly recommended that you speak with a certified public accountant regarding your specific tax situation for any scenarios you are considering.)

Step 2: Estimate an Expected Baseline, Income Growth Rate

This step is designed to help develop an estimate of the expected changes in income associated with annual raises or promotions. For this step, you will want to select a growth rate that can be realistically sustained (or averaged) over a ten-year time horizon. This time horizon may seem a bit excessive, but it is required to appropriately establish your baseline and compare it to potential MBA alternatives. Estimating a long-term compensation growth rate might seem difficult to estimate and ultimately somewhat subjective. (Ideally you would do this exercise for your entire career if the figures could be reasonably estimated.) Use your best judgment and consider historical salary increases and available benchmarks (e.g., other employees or friends at your current or similar employers). In this example, the baseline salary growth rate is estimated at 5 percent, reflecting a relatively aggressive career progression with significant advancement opportunities. This growth rate will ultimately be applied to your baseline income to determine the long-term overall compensation level you could expect if you were not pursuing an MBA investment.

Step 3: Calculate Your Total MBA-Related Spending

As discussed earlier in this chapter, a spending estimate for MBA options should include all costs attributable to the MBA that you would not be incurring if you were to continue with your baseline scenario. Such costs include GMAT entrance exam costs and study aid materials; graduate school application fees; campus visits; tuition; books and other study materials (including office supplies, computer hardware and software), as well as additional transportation or travel expenditures; and any relocation costs if a move is required. In this particular example, I have assembled a table of the expected costs associated with both a part-time and full-time sample MBA program.

	Part-Time (1 yr weekend MBA)	Full-Time MBA (2 yrs)
GMAT & study aids	$ 500	$ 500
Tuition	$ 30,000	$ 40,000
Books	$ 800	$ 1,000
Computer	$ 1,200	$ 1,200
Office supplies	$ 500	$ 500
Travel	$ 2,500	$ 2,500
Relocation	$ -	$ 10,000
Total	$ 35,500	$ 55,700

Step 4: Estimate Your Post-MBA Income

Estimating your income at the completion of an MBA program might seem like a daunting challenge at this point. However, it is a critical component to determining whether an MBA investment will make sound financial sense. A post-MBA salary will generally depend on the functional discipline that you pursue, the industry you're focusing on, and how much experience you had in each of these areas before you received your MBA. There are numerous resources to help you estimate a post-MBA income.

If you are currently in school, your campus career office is a good place to start. Many college career offices maintain records of the starting salaries (self-reported) of individuals graduating with MBAs, as well as other relevant information that can provide a benchmark. Internet job boards are also a good resource for estimating income with an MBA. Recruiters with whom you might have already developed a relationship should be able to provide additional perspective. In any of these situations, be certain to collect multiple data points and be certain that your work experience and other credentials match the job requirements so that your estimates are reasonable.

116

Building on the previous fictitious example, let's assume that an MBA program (whether a one-year or two-year, full-time program) provides a salary increase of $25,000 to $100,000 ($67,000 after taxes), as well as a $20,000 signing bonus ($13,400 after taxes).

Step 5: Estimate Your Post-MBA Income Growth Rate

Similar to the work you did to estimate a growth rate on your baseline income, you will need to estimate the expected rate of change (or ongoing growth rate) in your income after receiving an MBA. If you are planning to continue working at your existing employer after receiving your MBA, then this exercise is relatively straightforward. However, if you are looking to change employers or enter a new career discipline, then developing an estimate of compensation increases may be a bit more challenging. In either scenario, you should identify key roles along your desired and expected career ladder for the next ten years, considering the likely time between these roles. (You may find it helpful to reference the career map that you assembled in chapter 2: "Goal Setting and Management," as a starting point.) With your expected career and compensation path mapped out, you should then work to validate your compensation assumptions. Internet job boards such as Monster.com, Careerbuilder.com, theLadders.com, and 6figurejobs.com can be helpful for confirming your assumptions on compensation for different levels on your career map. If you use one of these sources to help validate your compensation assumptions for different roles and levels on your career map, just make sure that the companies and jobs referenced are in similar industries, the roles have similar responsibilities, and that the general requirements are consistent with your career map assumptions. (This will ensure that your compensation expectations are reasonable.)

Once you are comfortable with your career map and have validated the compensation expectations, you can use this information to back into salary growth rates. As an example, let's assume that you aspire to the role of director of marketing, but expect to start as a brand manager after receiving your MBA. Let's also assume that you determined (through discussions with peers and your research on job boards) that a director of marketing generally has five years of additional experience beyond a brand manager. Further, compensation for a director of marketing is estimated to be approximately $35,000 higher than a brand manager ($135,000 versus $100,000). With this information, you can estimate the compound annual growth as follows:

$(\$135,000 \ / \ \$100,000)^{(1/5)}-1 \ = \ 6.2$ percent, or generically as follows:

(ending salary / staring salary)$^{(1 \ / \ \text{number of years between starting and ending salary})}$ - 1

Just to keep the math simple, for this fictitious example, a 6.2 percent annual growth rate has been assumed in post-MBA income over each year of the ten-year time horizon. However, for your career map, you will want to use the process to calculate the growth rate in expected compensation between each role for the ten-year time frame (i.e., you may want to calculate growth rates that differ by role changes). This process will not

118

only ensure that you have an accurate estimate of your post-MBA income, but may also highlight critical compensation curve inflection points. If there is a dramatic compensation increase once a certain level is attained, you may want to independently develop a plan that accelerates your timeline to achieve this role.

Step 6: Calculate the Probable Value of an Alternative Investment

Recognizing that there are significant time and financial investments generally required in order to earn an MBA, a valuable question to consider is: What could alternatively be accomplished if you were to redeploy your time and money toward a different objective? If you are already on a reasonably strong career path, an alternative to the MBA might be investing greater time in your current job or in training toward specific development needs. Alternatively, it could be an investment in network development or job searching.

Recall the additional time investment associated with your MBA investment that you estimated in the beginning of the chapter in the "Opportunity Costs" section. Consider what the impact would be if you were to put an additional twenty-five hundred hours (or whatever you estimated the time investment of an MBA to be for your situation) towards an alternative objective. Whatever the best alternative scenario may be, you should try to estimate the financial benefit that you believe you could attain if you were to redeploy your planned MBA efforts toward your current situation.

In the example illustrated earlier, let's make the assumption that by focusing more on your current job (putting in more hours to take on additional responsibilities; leading more projects, etc.; and investing your own money against focused training costing $15,000 over a ten-year time period) that you could achieve an additional 2 percent in annual compensation through greater recognition and faster promotions over the next ten years. While this is a fairly simplistic assumption for this example, you may be able to reasonably estimate this for your situation. By assessing the different salary increases that you can expect through better annual ratings, or estimating how much faster you would get promoted (and the increased compensation associated with this), you can develop an updated career map that reflects the associated compensation curve.

Step 7: Assemble and Analyze the Financials on Your Potential MBA Investment

Now it is time to put all of the information you have calculated together to compare the value of each of the different alternatives. I recommend constructing a ten-year summary of the expected financials associated with each MBA scenario (scenario 1: part-time; scenario 2: full-time, etc.), then compare these scenarios against the baseline (what you would do if you were not pursuing an MBA), as well as an alternative investment (expected income if you were to invest your time and money into your current job, with additional focused training or other job development, rather than an MBA).

Baseline Income Projection

Start by building a summary of the baseline income scenario, using the after-tax, base salary estimate developed in step 1, then apply the income growth rate estimated in step 2 to extend the income stream out through ten years. It is a good idea to also include a cumulative total alongside the annual income stream. This will be helpful when comparing to other scenarios and estimating payback timelines. Below is an illustration (Figure 1) of "baseline" financials from the previously constructed example. (A $75,000 annual income is assumed in year one (from step 1), with annual income growth estimated at 5 percent (from step 2), and taxed at 33 percent.)

Figure 1: Baseline Income

Year	Current Job Salary	Annual Growth Rate	Projected Annual Salary	Tax Rate	After-Tax Annual Income	Cumulative
1	$ 75,000		$ 75,000	33%	$ 50,250	$ 50,250
2		5%	78,750	33%	52,763	103,013
3		5%	82,688	33%	55,401	158,413
4		5%	86,822	33%	58,171	216,584
5		5%	91,163	33%	61,079	277,663
6		5%	95,721	33%	64,133	341,796
7		5%	100,507	33%	67,340	409,136
8		5%	105,533	33%	70,707	479,843
9		5%	110,809	33%	74,242	554,085
10		5%	116,350	33%	77,954	632,039
					$ 632,039	

MBA Income Projections

Next, develop a similar matrix for each of the MBA scenarios. Start by including any income that will continue during your MBA program. Reference the work you did in

121

step 3 to estimate the costs of the MBA from a pure spending standpoint. Include this as a spending outlay in the first year (and potentially into the second year if it is a two-year program). Then, include the expected post-MBA income (estimated in step 4), beginning at the conclusion of your MBA. Reflect any estimated growth with your post-MBA income over the ten-year time horizon (calculated in step 5).

As an example, below are illustrations of the financials associated with the two fictitious MBA program scenarios from earlier in the chapter. To simplify this illustration, the calculation has been broken down into two parts. Part 1 involves the development of after-tax income assumptions on ordinary income (signing bonuses are excluded from this step). Part 2 involves the assembling of each of the after-tax items into a matrix that will allow us to compare this option against the baseline and alternative investment scenarios.

Part-Time MBA

In the first example (part-time MBA), year one has income from working at the current job of $75,000 (from step 1). Upon completing the MBA, annual income is expected to jump to $100,000 (from step 4), with an annual income growth of 6.2 percent through year ten (calculated in step 6). All income is taxed at 33 percent each year to arrive at after-tax projections. (Figure 2 has a matrix that illustrates the calculation and assembly of this information.)

Year	Current Job Salary	Post-MBA Salary	Annual Growth Rate	Projected Annual Salary	Tax Rate	After-Tax Annual Income	Cumulative
1	$ 75,000			$ 75,000	33%	$ 50,250	$ 50,250
2		$ 100,000		100,000	33%	67,000	117,250
3			6.2%	106,200	33%	71,154	188,404
4			6.2%	112,784	33%	75,566	263,970
5			6.2%	119,777	33%	80,251	344,220
6			6.2%	127,203	33%	85,226	429,446
7			6.2%	135,090	33%	90,510	519,956
8			6.2%	143,465	33%	96,122	616,078
9			6.2%	152,360	33%	102,081	718,160
10			6.2%	161,807	33%	108,410	826,570
						$ 826,570	

With the part-time MBA, costs of $35,500 were assumed (from step 3). (Note that many educational costs can be written off against taxes on ordinary income.) For simplicity, in this example it has been assumed that 100 percent of the education costs could offset ordinary income and therefore reduce the net impact by the effective income tax rate, assumed at 33 percent, to $23,785 ($35,500 x (1 – 33%)). Recall that in this example, it was assumed that you would receive a $20,000 signing bonus in the new job after you completed the MBA program. After taxes of 33 percent, this reduces the overall benefit to $13,400.

Combining each of the relevant items on an after-tax basis (see the illustration in Figure 3) will provide the net benefit expected over the course of the ten-year time horizon and provide a quantitative perspective on the value of the part-time MBA investment.

Year	Ordinary Income	Signing Bonus	MBA Outlays	Total Income	Cumulative
1	$ 50,250		$ (23,785)	$ 26,465	$ 26,465
2	67,000	$ 13,400		80,400	106,865
3	71,154			71,154	178,019
4	75,566			75,566	253,585
5	80,251			80,251	333,835
6	85,226			85,226	419,061
7	90,510			90,510	509,571
8	96,122			96,122	605,693
9	102,081			102,081	707,775
10	108,410			108,410	816,185
	$ 826,570	$ 13,400	$ (23,785)	$ 816,185	

Full-Time MBA

In the second example (full-time MBA), there is no income during the time the individual is attending the MBA program. Upon completing the MBA, annual income is expected to jump to $100,000 (from step 4), with an annual income growth of 6.2 percent through year ten (calculated in step 6). All ordinary income is taxed at 33 percent each year to arrive at after-tax projections. (Figure 4 has a matrix that illustrates the calculation and assembly of this information.)

124

Figure 4: Full-Time MBA

Year	Current Job Salary	Post-MBA Salary	Annual Growth Rate	Projected Annual Salary	Tax Rate	After-Tax Annual Income	Cumulative
1				$ -		$ -	$ -
2				-		-	-
3		$ 100,000		100,000	33%	67,000	67,000
4			6.2%	106,200	33%	71,154	138,154
5			6.2%	112,784	33%	75,566	213,720
6			6.2%	119,777	33%	80,251	293,970
7			6.2%	127,203	33%	85,226	379,196
8			6.2%	135,090	33%	90,510	469,706
9			6.2%	143,465	33%	96,122	565,828
10			6.2%	152,360	33%	102,081	667,910
						$ 667,910	

With the full-time MBA, costs of $55,700 were assumed (from step 3) for the entire two-year program. Similar to the assumptions made for the part-time MBA program, it is assumed that 100 percent of the full-time MBA costs can offset ordinary income, and as a further simplifying assumption, that there is other income or taxes due by this individual that the educational expenses can offset. (The income tax offset is reflected in this example in years one and two, but in reality may be offset against income in future periods as well depending on your income.) Therefore, the effective costs of the education would be $37,319 ($55,700 x (1 – 33%)), or $18,660 per year for two years based on a tax rate of 33 percent. Similar to the part-time MBA, if you received a $20,000 signing bonus in the new job following the MBA, this would equal $13,400 after taxes.

The combination of ordinary income, MBA costs, and the signing bonus associated with the job are summarized on an after-tax basis in Figure 5.

Figure 5: Full-Time MBA (After-Tax Summary)

Year	Ordinary Income	Signing Bonus	MBA Outlays	Total Income	Cumulative
1	$ -		$ (18,660)	$ (18,660)	$ (18,660)
2	-		(18,660)	(18,660)	(37,319)
3	67,000	$ 13,400		80,400	43,081
4	71,154			71,154	114,235
5	75,566			75,566	189,801
6	80,251			80,251	270,051
7	85,226			85,226	355,277
8	90,510			90,510	445,787
9	96,122			96,122	541,909
10	102,081			102,081	643,991
	$ 667,910	$ 13,400	$ (37,319)	$ 643,991	

Alternative Investment Income Projection

In a manner similar to how you summarized the baseline and MBA scenarios, you should organize the work done in step 6 to develop the value of your income stream if you were to invest the time and money planned for an MBA into other areas that could help benefit your career. Below is an illustration of financials from an "alternative investment," using the example developed in step 6. (Identical to the "baseline" income, a $75,000 annual salary is assumed in year one (from step 1), with an annual income growth estimated at 5 percent (from step 2), and taxed at 33 percent. However, the incremental income growth of 2 percent (from step 6) is added, making the annual income growth rate now 7 percent.) (See Figure 6.)

Figure 6: Alternative Investment

Year	Current Job Salary	Annual Growth Rate	Projected Annual Salary	Tax Rate	After-Tax Annual Income	Cumulative
1	$ 75,000		$ 75,000	33%	$ 50,250	$ 50,250
2		7%	80,250	33%	53,768	104,018
3		7%	85,868	33%	57,531	161,549
4		7%	91,878	33%	61,558	223,107
5		7%	98,310	33%	65,867	288,975
6		7%	105,191	33%	70,478	359,453
7		7%	112,555	33%	75,412	434,865
8		7%	120,434	33%	80,691	515,555
9		7%	128,864	33%	86,339	601,894
10		7%	137,884	33%	92,383	694,277
					$ 694,277	

Recall that $15,000 of staggered investments in training or other development was estimated to accelerate career growth in the alternative investment scenario. (This equates to $10,050 after applying a 33% tax rate.) Combining the after-tax investments with the after-tax income by year, a complete view of the alternative investment scenario can be derived. (Figure 7 provides a financial summary of this scenario.)

127

Figure 7: Alternative Investment (After-Tax Summary)

Year	Ordinary Income	Investment Outlays	Total Income	Cumulative
1	$ 50,250	$ (3,350)	$ 46,900	$ 46,900
2	53,768		53,768	$ 100,668
3	57,531	$ (3,350)	54,181	$ 154,849
4	61,558		61,558	$ 216,407
5	65,867		65,867	$ 282,275
6	70,478		70,478	$ 352,753
7	75,412	$ (3,350)	72,062	$ 424,815
8	80,691		80,691	$ 505,505
9	86,339		86,339	$ 591,844
10	92,383		92,383	$ 684,227
	$ 694,277	$ (10,050)	$ 684,227	

Now that the ten-year financial projections have been calculated for each scenario, it is possible to effectively compare the different options against the baseline to assess the relative value of each. The matrix (illustrated in Figure 8) provides a summary of the different options evaluated in the aforementioned example.

Figure 8: Option Comparisons (After-Tax)

Year	Baseline Income Annual	Baseline Income Cumulative	Part-Time MBA Annual	Part-Time MBA Cumulative	Full-Time MBA Annual	Full-Time MBA Cumulative	Alternative Investment Annual	Alternative Investment Cumulative
1	$ 50,250	$ 50,250	$ 26,465	$ 26,465	$ (18,660)	$ (18,660)	$ 46,900	$ 46,900
2	52,763	103,013	80,400	106,865	(18,660)	(37,319)	53,768	100,668
3	55,401	158,413	71,154	178,019	80,400	43,081	54,181	154,849
4	58,171	216,584	75,566	253,585	71,154	114,235	61,558	216,407
5	61,079	277,663	80,251	333,835	75,566	189,801	65,867	282,275
6	64,133	341,796	85,226	419,061	80,251	270,051	70,478	352,753
7	67,340	409,136	90,510	509,571	85,226	355,277	72,062	424,815
8	70,707	479,843	96,122	605,693	90,510	445,787	80,691	505,505
9	74,242	554,085	102,081	707,775	96,122	541,909	86,339	591,844
10	77,954	632,039	108,410	816,185	102,081	643,991	92,383	684,227
	$ 632,039		$ 816,185		$ 643,991		$ 684,227	
Difference vs. Baseline:			$ 184,146		$ 11,952		$ 52,187	

In this particular example, it is clear when comparing the cumulative net after-tax income from each option that the part-time MBA provides the greatest expected overall financial benefit, with more than $815K in net income versus just over $630K with the baseline option. The next best financial option is investing the time and money planned for an MBA in alternative career investments. It is estimated that this would provide nearly $685K in net income. The least attractive option in this example is to maintain the current plan (i.e., the baseline scenario).

You will likely find it useful to continue to analyze the scenarios by looking at the cumulative net income provided each year. This will allow you to see how quickly an investment provides a relative payback. In dissecting this example, you will see that the part-time MBA is not only the best option, but that it provides an estimated net benefit in year two over all the other options, including the baseline (see the cumulative income shaded in year two for the part-time MBA, which is higher than all the other options at this time period). The part-time MBA option becomes increasingly better as a choice in each subsequent year, adjusting for one-time impacts, such as signing bonuses.

A graphical summary is also very useful in identifying trends (see Figure 9). Of particular note in this example is the relative value of a full-time MBA. When evaluated over a ten-year time horizon, the full-time MBA is not much better than the baseline option. However, the higher overall compensation rate will ultimately make this scenario more attractive if the timeline were extended further. Another trend that becomes more apparent when examined graphically is the growing benefits of the part-time MBA versus the alternative investment (you can see the slope of the part-time MBA become increasingly steep compared to the alternative investment as the timeline is extended).

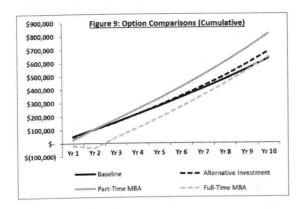

Please recognize that the conclusions drawn in this example were purely for illustrative purposes. You will need to adjust the assumptions for your unique situation in order to appropriately evaluate your opportunities and develop an accurate financial valuation of your different options. (To simplify this process, an "MBA valuation calculator" is available for download on the *Active Career Management* website at www.activecareermanagement.com and provides a structured framework to value a potential MBA investment against different alternatives.)

As you examine your own situation, taking a quantitative approach similar to the one outlined in this chapter should help ensure that you make the best financial decision and eliminate emotion from the decision-making process as much as possible. When assessing different options, recognize that most assumptions (particularly long-term estimates such as

130

compensation growth rates) will likely have a fair degree of uncertainty in terms of what you can expect. Therefore, it is advisable to take this into consideration when assessing the ultimate output and comparing one option versus another. For those variables with a range of possible outputs, you might find it helpful to run multiple scenarios with different outputs to determine how sensitive the overall conclusion is to that particular variable before committing to a specific career path.

Finally, if you happen to have a financial background, you might also want to consider adjusting the annual after-tax net income by an appropriate discount rate in order to account for the time value of money.

Developing a Plan to Exploit Your MBA Investment

If you are already in an MBA program or have gone through the exercises earlier in this chapter and believe that an MBA investment would provide you with career value, then it is very important that you have a plan to exploit this significant investment. As a starting point, you should have a clear understanding of exactly what you want to achieve with your MBA and develop a plan to realize this goal.

Recognize that earning your MBA is not just about the grades or about the grade point average associated with your time in school. This is an opportunity for you to develop the skills that will enable you to gain the leadership, technical capabilities, or diversification of experience, as well as network of contacts, that you will need to succeed when you enter or reenter the workforce. If you are at this point in your career or educational journey, I strongly recommend that you

131

consider rereading chapter 1: "Maximizing Your Education," paying particular attention to the section called "How to Use What You Study." This should provide some perspective on how to exploit your time in school to help you achieve your goals and ultimately ensure you earn the desired return on your investment—both in time and money.

Chapter 15
Why and When to Change Jobs

Changing jobs is rarely easy and is not something to do without careful consideration. However, sometimes this is the best (and only option) if you want to continue to progress on your desired career path. This might be particularly true if advancement opportunities or new resume-building experiences are limited at your current employer. The key is being able to carefully and rationally assess the career path and compensation outlook at your current employer versus alternatives, then know when to make a move (and make the commitment to actually change when you find a better opportunity). This chapter introduces a logical, seven-part, systematic approach that you can use to evaluate your current employment outlook against other alternatives, while independently highlighting some less quantifiable factors to consider.

Step 1: Confirm Where You Want to Be and by When

Before going too far down the decision-making process on whether to consider a new employer, first calibrate your progress against the career milestones and goals you have already set for yourself. (It might be helpful to reference the career map document that you assembled in chapter 2: "Goal Setting and Management" at this time.) If you have not assembled a map of what positions you want to attain and the approximate time frame, then you should consider assembling one now. Be sure to include in your timeline the different role levels, key responsibilities, skill set development, and learning objectives (ideally those that are applicable at your current employer *and* to external organizations), as well as realistic compensation. (Note that titles are often not comparable across different organizations. Therefore, make sure you clearly define your expectations on other factors, particularly when trying to calibrate your progress and career path options in different companies.)

Step 2: Contemplate Your Progress against Key Milestones

After completing and updating your career map, consider how you are progressing against each of your milestones you targeted at this point in your career journey. (Contemplate all the following areas: title, responsibilities, relevant skills, and compensation.) If you are moving at your desired pace, then it may be worth pausing to consider what is driving you to think about an external opportunity—this is not to suggest that there are not good reasons to look for more aggressive career growth opportunities elsewhere—but just to emphasize that you should not necessarily discount your current employer if prospects there are highly compelling.

It is in this step where an external peer network can be incredibly useful to calibrate your current progress versus external potential progress. (Chapter 3: "Building a Network: Who to Know and Why," provides an overview of the art and science to creating and maintaining a professional network, and also includes some thoughts on how to leverage this to your advantage.) Calibrating yourself against others with similar goals and aspirations

134

on career progress can be very helpful to assess your milestones and progress. If you do not have a strong network, it might be helpful (although not optimal) to simply look at other individuals in your field. You might even be able to reference individuals at your current employer (this should definitely be relatively easy to benchmark) who have rapidly advanced and compare their career progress against the pace at which you are tracking. Even if you are on track with your targeted performance milestones, this does not mean that you should not consider new opportunities—particularly if there is more upside career growth at other employers. (This will be explored further in steps 3 through 6.)

If you are *not* advancing according to your career map targets, then there are two important questions to consider, as follows:

> *1). Why are you not moving as fast as expected?*
> *2). Do you have reason to believe that this trajectory will change?*

Regarding the first question, consider your performance trajectory versus your peers, in addition to your previously developed career map—both can be very relevant benchmarks. In answering the question of "Why are you not moving as fast as expected?", it is important that you work to truly understand the root cause(s). (Be honest with yourself about the potential root cause(s) and what you can control—even indirectly; it is the best way to make sure that you address the issue(s) and avoid hitting similar roadblocks in the future.) In addition to your introspective assessment, ask for feedback from others— peers, current and former managers, as well as mentors or coaches—and gather advice about what you could reasonably do to get onto your targeted career path.

The second question was "Do you have reason to believe that this (career) trajectory will change?". There can indeed be legitimate reasons why career advancement might slow at certain points without being a major concern, such as natural organizational bottlenecks. However, make certain you understand whether such a situation truly exists, what it will take for you to break through this bottleneck, and what the "triggers" are for you to reassess this situation and when. In my experience, this is the point where many individuals lose control of their career progression—and it is entirely avoidable. Particularly if you prefer to continue working for your current employer, consider what would realistically cause your trajectory to change if you are not on the desired trajectory now. Assess the degree of reasonableness associated with such scenarios. At the same time, it is critical to set some specific milestones or decision points when you will reevaluate your situation. Getting complacent with a "wait and see" attitude while falling behind a targeted career path progression is a common and potentially very costly career mistake. A good way to mitigate this situation is being mindful of this risk and open to reconsidering your career options if advancement doesn't occur as planned.

Step 3: Assess Your Sponsorship Relative to the Competition

One element of career advancement that is often inappropriately valued is the level of sponsorship required to advance one's career—especially at higher levels in an organization. This point is relevant not only to assess the sponsorship needed with your current employer but also when contemplating what would be required to advance at a new employer. To appropriately evaluate your sponsorship, you may find it useful to consider the following questions:

> 1). What is your level of sponsorship?
> 2). Who are the sponsors needed to advance to the levels you desire in the organization?
> 3). Who is your relevant competition for future targeted roles on your career map?
> 4). What is the level of sponsorship of your internal competition and what does this mean to you?

What is Your Level of Sponsorship?

Understanding the level of sponsorship you have is crucial to making an informed decision regarding career plans at your current employer. I recommend starting by simply asking your manager and mentor (if you have one) to directly provide some candid perspective on the level of sponsorship that you have within the organization. If you are told that your sponsorship level is not as significant as expected or as strong as needed for advancement, then at least you are aware up front and you can assess what it may take to change this—and whether it is reasonable or realistic on your targeted advancement timeline. However, even if you receive positive feedback, you will want to validate this.

One method for validating your level of sponsorship is to examine your recent career history at your current employer. Start by asking yourself a few questions. Have any roles become open recently that you had targeted as part of your career map or for which you would have been a logical candidate? Were you asked to apply or interview for these opportunities? If you did get the opportunity to interview, what was the outcome? If you received an offer, this is a pretty good sign that you have sponsorship at least to this level in the organization. However, if you did not get an offer for the role, then understanding why you did not (or at least what you were told as the reason) will be helpful. The key question is whether or not this is what you should have expected if you indeed had a large degree of sponsorship. If you did not even get asked to apply or interview, then there is a separate question: "Why not?" Again, it is worth considering whether or not this is what should be expected for someone with a high degree of sponsorship (most likely it is *not*—but you will need to be the judge of this based on your particular situation).

Who are the Sponsors Needed to Advance to the Levels You Desire in the Organization?

When contemplating roles at your current employer, consider who will be the key decision makers, as well as what sponsorship you will require to attain this role and other higher-level job opportunities. Think about what is required to gain this sponsorship internally versus externally. If you already have much of the sponsorship you need and are advancing along your targeted career map as desired, then remaining at your current employer might be a pretty logical decision. However, if it seems unlikely that you will acquire the sponsorship you require for advancement internally, then you should consider what you need to advance along your desired path at an alternative employer.

Gaining sponsorship generally takes time, and you must produce repeated examples of strong results in different roles and projects. This is particularly critical to evaluate when you're thinking about new employment opportunities. In the new employment situation you're evaluating, consider what level of sponsorship you would need to advance to the targeted roles along your career map (and what it would take to advance, as well as how much time).

Who is Your Relevant Competition for Future Targeted Roles on Your Career Map?

Understanding how your sponsorship will play out can sometimes be fairly difficult to estimate—especially several roles into the future. However, thinking this through strategically and analytically will increase your chances of effectively predicting this and help you capitalize on the situation. As you advance in an organization, there are generally fewer roles available, and the time is often longer between promotional opportunities. Therefore, evaluating who else is competing for roles that you have targeted is another crucial variable. This assessment might be somewhat subjective in nature, based on who is in your peer group, and taking into account the known career aspirations of these other individuals. It is also worthwhile to give attention to more junior individuals who are advancing at accelerated rates who might not yet presently be in your peer group, but who could be competing for targeted future roles. Finally, depending on the organization where you work, externally sourced talent might be another source of competition to think about.

What is the Level of Sponsorship of Your Internal Competition and What Does This Mean to You?

Just as you assessed your own level of sponsorship, estimating the level of sponsorship of your peer group is another factor that should help you to determine your likelihood of progressing on the career path that you have outlined with your current employer. All else being equal, the greater the extent of sponsorship that your peers have, the more challenging it will be for you to attain your goals—simply due to the higher degree of competition. Assessing the sponsorship level of your peers can be done in the same way as you evaluated your own, recognizing that the available information will likely be even less clear.

To the extent that it is known, consider what roles your peers might have been interested in that became open. Were any of them seriously considered for these opportunities? If so, what was the outcome? If any of these individuals received job offers, then this validates that these individuals have sponsorship (at least through the particular level of the job they received). However, if these individuals did not even get asked to apply or interview (particularly if the position was filled with external talent), then this clearly highlights that there is something holding the individual(s) back, which does not bode incredibly well for his or her sponsorship. However, it may mean that your likelihood of advancement is higher, all else equal.

Considering your career goals in the context of sponsorship for yourself and potential internal competition should provide some very helpful career advancement perspectives when contemplating future opportunities at your current employer—particularly as you move up in an organization and higher-level roles become more scarce.

Step 4: Evaluate Your Prospects for the Next Two to Three Roles

Another factor to consider when contemplating whether to explore job opportunities outside of your existing company is an honest evaluation of your prospects for the next two to three likely career moves—and the associated timeline for achieving them. Thinking beyond your current or next role is of great consequence as you evaluate your career prospects and unfortunately something that is very frequently overlooked.

Predicting your next role (much less your next two to three roles) can be difficult. However, think back to your career map (from chapter 2) and where you are along this continuum. Considering your level of sponsorship (as examined in step 2), as well as your competition (internal and external, as evaluated in step 3), do your best to honestly predict where you see yourself in the next two to three roles at your current company—and how long it will take to progress there. This will clearly be a judgment call on your part, and there may be several permutations. However, try to assign a probability of occurrence to each scenario, focusing on the scenario with the highest likelihood. If there are other factors that will influence what roles you will likely attain (e.g., natural bottlenecks at future positions targeted in your career map; the level of company growth and associated implications on future role opportunities; general talent movement trends or timelines, etc.), be sure to include them in your projections.

After developing your most likely list of future roles, you will want to understand the key enablers to attaining these positions. This will likely include specific skills, experiences, demonstrated results, leadership, and sponsorship. Consider the challenges associated with each move and how long it will likely take to make these transitions within your current company. Finally, compare this against your career map roles and associated timeline to check for alignment. Ideally, your most likely internal career moves will match up closely with your previously developed career map from a role and timeline perspective. However, if you have major disconnects, then this is a sign that you might want to explore your prospects externally. (Step 5 will provide perspective on how to effectively compare your projected internal role progression—both roles and timing—against likely external scenarios to help provide some context on whether your advancement expectations at your current company seem appropriate.)

If, while going through this exercise, you do not foresee the opportunity for significant advancement over the course of your next two to three roles (or you do not believe there will even be opportunities for two to three different assignments at your current company), then this is definitely a sign that you should at least explore external employment options. Timing might be a consideration, especially if there are specific skills that you can gain at your current company that will be critical to have before entertaining an external search. If there are skills that you

142

truly believe are critical to attain before leaving, be honest with yourself about how likely it is that you will be able to attain these at your current company and how long it will take to acquire them. Also, consider whether there might be other ways to gain these skills (e.g., executive education). If you are in this situation, just be certain you have a clear plan to acquire these skills, with a timeline for completing this, as well as "trigger points" for starting an external job search.

Step 5: Assess Your External Options to Advance at a Faster Rate

In contemplating whether to change employers, be sure to assess your prospects for advancement for the next two to three roles with different, prospective employers. Essentially, you are evaluating upside potential at outside employers versus your current one (and the probability of this happening). This is a critical test that individuals often miss in the employer evaluation process (particularly if the compensation is significantly different), but one that can have major ramifications on long-term, career advancement prospects.

Changing companies might indeed provide different and better future prospects, especially if the new company is growing at a more rapid rate, or if the culture and needs are more aligned to your style and talents. However, be mindful that sponsorship generally takes time to develop—often even more so in a new organization with different customers. This might be mitigated to some degree if you already have a network of sponsors at the new organization that you acquired from previous work experiences. With this in mind, think through not only what you could logically expect to do next and on what schedule, but also what the key enablers would be to attain these future positions (including the results you will need to deliver, the sponsorship required, skill development, etc.).

Match up the career paths for the next two to three roles at your current company (step 4) versus the outside companies you're considering (step 5), comparing requirements, expected advancement timeline, sponsorship requirements, and risks, as well as the opportunities associated with the different roles at each company (including the challenges associated with taking on new roles versus potentially staying motivated if the pace of change or advancement is expected to be different between companies). In doing this evaluation, you will also want to consider the impacts that the different roles at each respective company would have on your resume at a future date (e.g., the responsibilities of each role, size of the business or team that you would be responsible for, total compensation, and the career flexibility that is provided by the experiences you would gain and the reputation of the company).

After completing this comparison between your potential internal versus external career path, you should have a good sense of which path provides the best prospects. The next step is to test this conclusion with external data and information to confirm it before making the decision to either continue with your current company or make a change.

Step 6: Gain External Validation for Your Proposed Decision before Executing It

Before making the decision to either stay with your current employer or change to a different organization, you definitely want to get some external perspective on your thinking. Although the process outlined in steps 1 through 5 should help to reduce the level of emotion in making this decision, contemplating a company change is very difficult for most people—especially if you have been with your current company for a long time.

Don't forget to gain perspective on how your career path will be valued in the external marketplace, outside of the organizations you are presently evaluating. This is where your external network of colleagues and trusted recruiters is invaluable.

Begin by making a list of colleagues in your network with similar career aspirations (refer to chapter 3: "Building a Network: Who to know and Why," if helpful). Focus on those individuals who are ideally on a more accelerated career path than you and whose guidance you can trust. It is also useful to include external recruiters with whom you have a relationship and who have experience placing individuals at higher levels (than where you are at today) in different organizations.

To make certain that the discussions you are having with these individuals are as productive and as unbiased as possible, you should create a structured framework that will facilitate consistent conversations with each individual. The process that you have already followed in steps 1 through 5 in this chapter will provide a good foundation and background for initiating these discussions. A primary focus should be feedback on the paths outlined in step 5, with special consideration for the longer-range implications of your different organizational choices in the overall market. Job dimensions such as team management, the size of the business supported, the size of the team and the scope of their work, the number of levels between your role and the CEO, as well as compensation, can all have a bearing on how career moves are viewed by potential employers. All else being equal, you will want to be able to show increasing scope of management and responsibilities—even when changing organizations. So, changes that materially impact these factors should be carefully evaluated and discussed.

To further validate your thinking, it can be helpful to evaluate the experience and other dimensions listed for various positions on different internal and external job boards. Try to focus on positions that you would target in the next two to three moves, and examine what is expected for an *ideal* candidate in terms of experience. Consider whether the roles that you are evaluating at your current or other prospective employers will be realistically providing you with the experiences you need to attain roles such as these (and that these experiences truly apply in the outside market). This is a good final test to ensure that whatever positions you are considering make sense, and that you have a plan to gain the experiences necessary (on a reasonable time frame) to attain your objectives.

Step 7: Make the Decision

Once you have completed the organization evaluation process and appropriately validated your thinking externally, it is time to make your decision. At this point, the best plan is to make the decision and act on it. Whether the decision is to stick with your current company or make a change, you should avoid the temptation to second-guess your thinking once you have decided. Instead, you should embrace the path forward, knowing that you have done an appropriate assessment and are making the right decision based on the options and information you have available.

If you decide to stay with your current employer, make sure that you have a plan to continue to gain the experiences and build the sponsorship you need to progress to the next level. (Recognize that you will want to build skills and experiences that will be marketable not just internally but also at other employers.) Continue to update your career map, setting clear goals for what you want to achieve and by when. Periodically assessing your progress, and considering how and to what extent your responsibilities and experiences are building your resume for future progression, according to your long-term career objectives, should continue to be a priority to ensure that your current employer still provides the best future prospects.

If you decide that changing employers is the appropriate action, carefully consider how you can make the transition as seamless as possible for your current employer to avoid "burning bridges" that you might regret later. This involves providing at least two weeks written notice of your intention to leave and finishing any work that you agreed to complete prior to leaving. Beyond providing a common courtesy to your current employer and coworkers, this will help to minimize any adverse reactions that your leaving might create. This is important—particularly if you are going to a company in the same industry—as you might find yourself working with some of the same individuals at a future time and will want to make certain that your exit does not create any awkwardness.

147

Regardless of your level or position, when you start a role at a new employer, making a good first impression is incredibly important. Gaining sponsorship with influential leaders at your new employer is critical to advance at the rate you desired and expected with your move. As an experienced external hire, the expectations will generally be very high. Therefore, before starting a job with a new company, it is recommended that you build a "one-hundred-day plan" that involves specific objectives and milestones that you can frequently check yourself against. (It is okay to change direction once you start if you find that some of your assumptions were not totally accurate.) Once you start with a new company, make a commitment to "overinvest" to get "up-to-speed" as rapidly as possible, working to make noticeable and significant improvements to the new organization. (Along these lines, you might find it helpful to review chapter 9: "How and Why to Impress Customers Early", chapter 10: "Building and Exploiting Exposure to Gain Sponsorship", and chapter 11: "Managing Perceptions.")

Chapter 16
Continuous Performance Assessment
and Management

The final, critical element of "active career management" involves implementing and adhering to a process to continuously assess your performance and progress against your current job and career objectives—and to then manage your future actions against this assessment. Just as effectively managing an important project involves starting with the development of a detailed project plan with key milestones, timelines, owners, and clear accountabilities, and then frequently checking on progress and adjusting plans accordingly—your own career management should be no different.

While there are certain elements of your career management that you should assess on a monthly, weekly, or even daily basis—I would recommend assessing your progress against overall career milestones on a quarterly basis. You should also assess your performance against the objectives of your current job on the same time frame. More frequent assessment can potentially result in overthinking your daily activities relative to your long-range career map and runs the risk of you losing the appropriate focus you need for your current job responsibilities. An annual assessment process is a bit too long to wait—especially because achieving the annual objectives of your current role affects your future advancement.

Building on the content in prior chapters, your assessment of your current job and career performance should consider the following factors:

1). An *honest*, personal assessment of your performance against current job objectives.
2). Perspective on others' opinions or perceptions of your performance.
3). Ramifications of your current work against longer-range, career options.

Honest Assessment of Performance against Current Job Objectives

A strong performance against your current job objectives is absolutely necessary for progressing against your career map milestones. Therefore, you must frequently (ideally, quarterly) assess your progress against your current job objectives—even if the work is not yet complete. (Consider the discussion in chapter 9: "How and Why to Impress Customers Early," on the importance of making a good initial impression to create and maintain a positive "halo effect.") Doing an honest, no excuses, personal assessment of your progress against your current job objectives is the first step in a continuous performance assessment and management process.

If your performance is not where *you* would like it to be—recognizing that this might still mean that you are performing in line with *normal* job expectations—consider what it would take to get your performance on track. As much as possible, try to distance yourself from any emotional elements that could cloud your thinking or judgment and objectively assess your objectives, where you would like to be, and what you would need to happen to attain them. Focus on those elements that you can control or influence, and try to avoid any temptation to make excuses or fixate on those external, political, or other factors that affect your performance but are out of your direct control. Similar to the discussion on overall career management in chapter 2: "Goal Setting and Management," start with the end in mind as it relates to your current-year performance goals (i.e., what you would like to have achieved by year-end, as well as your next quarterly check-in), and work your way backward, building-out those enablers that are required to achieve your goals. Set clear, measurable expectations for each—including milestones with timelines, owners, accountabilities, and plans for what you will do if this plan is not working at your next assessment point.

Even if your performance seems to be very strong, there is always an opportunity for some improvement. Challenge yourself to consider what the "next level" of performance would look like if you did not have any constraints—then consider what it would take to achieve this. Even if this is not practical, it is a good exercise to make sure you are thinking about what "exceptional" or "world class" looks like and to continue to aspire for greater performance.

Perspective on Others' Opinions or Perceptions of Your Performance

In addition to providing an honest personal assessment of your performance and building a plan that addresses any gaps or opportunities for improvement that you see, it is incredibly valuable to consider how others view your performance against current objectives, too. Clearly, you should consider your current manager's assessment. However, per the discussions in chapters 10 and 11 on managing perceptions and building sponsorship, you should also give significant consideration to the perceptions that were created with targeted sponsors as a result of your current performance.

As you contemplate changes in how you approach your job objectives, first try to understand whether your immediate manager and targeted sponsors are aware of the work that you are doing. Secondly, you should consider how this work is being perceived. If your work is getting a lot of exposure, then understanding how it is being perceived may be fairly clear. However, sometimes getting this perspective is not as transparent—particularly if there is not a high level of awareness of you or your work, for whatever reason. In these situations, directly asking for feedback is a good option. Start with your manager, but also consider getting feedback from some of your targeted sponsors, if you have a relationship that would warrant this type of open dialog. If you get some good, candid, thoughtful feedback, be prepared to incorporate this into your work plans—and be prepared to provide more frequent updates to your manager and those targeted sponsors from whom you have received feedback in this process. Remember, that how your work is viewed by your manager and influential leaders is incredibly critical to your advancement, particularly as you move up in an organization. Being mindful of the direct and indirect feedback that you receive, as well as how your work can impact the objectives of these leaders, should help you to shape the work that you are doing to attain maximum exposure, and ultimately sponsorship.

Ramifications of Your Current Work against Longer-Range Career Options

Clearly, your top priority is to make sure that your performance is on track against objectives in your current role, and that this is seen and valued by your manager and targeted sponsors. However, it is also worthwhile to consider the longer-term ramifications of the work that you are doing on future role opportunities. It might be necessary to adjust your approach to current work to develop 1) the appropriate skills, and 2) the confidence of influential leaders that you will need in the future in order to be successful. Striking this balance will make these leaders see you as the right individual to put into roles that you have targeted as part of your career map.

Being effective in your current role—even if you are recognized as a stand-out performer—will not by itself guarantee you get the opportunity to move into your next desired role. This is especially true if the perspective of your manager and other influential leaders is that your experiences are not sufficient or appropriate for advancement. Therefore, as you go through your quarterly performance assessment process, reference the career map that you developed in chapter 2: "Goal Setting and Management." Starting with the end in mind and working backward, reconsider what experiences and sponsorship you need to get to your targeted end-state career goal, and honestly assess how your current work might or might not support this. Whether your current role responsibilities align with your targeted future roles or not, there are always opportunities to increase the value of your work. However, particularly if you do not see a close alignment between your current work and your next several targeted career moves, then you should use this periodic assessment process to carefully evaluate how you can enhance or modify what you are doing to increase that alignment.

Modifying or realigning your current work to better support your long-range career goals might seem challenging or even potentially risky. However, you can mitigate this by realigning or modifying your work to create additional value to the organization, which will ultimately be supported by your manager and other key leaders.

As an example, when I was in a role as a fairly junior financial analyst, one of my responsibilities was to work with the business teams to develop the departmental budgets for the upcoming year. I understood that this work was important and provided a learning opportunity for me. However, I also recognized that even if I executed the activity flawlessly, it was unlikely to provide any significant reaction from potential future sponsors that would impact whether I received opportunities to progress to a more senior analyst or manager role in the future (my next career goals). However, by thinking creatively, I was able to come up with a way to both deliver the current year's objective while gaining exposure and sponsorship from some influential leaders who would not normally be interested in this fairly routine activity. In going through the early stages of meetings with departmental budget personnel, it became very clear to me that the tools these individuals had available were very limited and counterintuitive. This resulted in a great deal of frustration and inefficiency, as departmental personnel spent far too much time digging through a myriad of reports and systems to attempt to effectively manage their spending. Moreover, this phenomenon was prevalent throughout the company. I immediately saw this as an opportunity to not just build the budgets for the following year but also to develop a significant enhancement to the tools and techniques used by *all* departmental personnel to more effectively track and manage spending throughout the year. Although this activity took additional time on my part, I was able to realign my work (with the support of my manager) to something that significantly benefitted the company, while also increasing my level of exposure and sponsorship with leaders in my functional area. Further, this work highlighted my capability to operate at the "higher level" needed for advancement to some of the future roles targeted on my career map.

As you evaluate opportunities in your current role to redefine the work to ensure it provides you with the experiences and sponsorship that you need in order to be seriously considered for targeted future roles, recognize that this does not mean that you need to change everything about your current role. Often significant sponsorship is generated from just one or two major projects in a given year. Consider that in my example, the departmental budgeting work was just one element within my overall job responsibilities. I did not reengineer my entire job, but rather focused on one area that I believed I could improve to gain additional experience and ultimately demonstrate to potential sponsors that I could operate in higher-level jobs with greater responsibilities.

As you incorporate this type of "enhanced" work into your current objectives, be certain to use the same rigorous performance assessments against these "incremental" objectives as you would with your normal job responsibilities. (This is especially important if you have shared your plan with your manager or targeted

155

sponsors, who are now expecting to see this output on a specific timeline.) It is also worth noting that you cannot afford to let your *normal* job responsibilities suffer. Enhancing, modifying, or redefining your current objectives is likely to take additional effort—so be prepared for this, and recognize that you will need to realistically assess what you can do and by when.

Incorporating this opportunistic thinking into your periodic performance assessment and management process will be one additional element that will increase your likelihood of gaining the experiences, exposure and sponsorship that you will need to achieve your stretching career objectives. And the resulting products of your work should provide a win-win for both you and the organization you support!

Chapter 17
Some Final Thoughts

After completing this book, you should now be aware of (and hopefully use) a number of the techniques that will help you to more actively and effectively manage the development and advancement of your career. While there is no specific formula to achieving career success, having a clear plan and diligently managing it will increase this likelihood.

To be most useful, I would advise frequently referencing the chapters that apply to you as you progress along your personal career journey. This could be at critical milestones or decision points, such as if you are considering additional schooling or contemplating a company change. However, you will also likely find certain elements useful as you do your quarterly performance alignment check-ins.

To further help you in your career navigation, several interactive tools are available on the *Active Career Management* website at www.activecareermanagement.com. New tools and resources are frequently being added to help you in your career management process—so I would encourage you to check in frequently. You may also stay connected on Facebook at www.facebook.com/ActiveCareerManagement.

I truly hope you have and will continue to find this book to be a useful resource and wish you the best as you navigate your career journey.

56656065R00093

Made in the USA
San Bernardino, CA
13 November 2017